HEALTHY MEXICAN

REGIONAL COOKERY

A Culinary Travelogue

LOTTE MENDELSOHN

Font & Center Press
P.O. Box 95
Weston, MA 02193

Published by
Font & Center Press
P.O. Box 95
Weston, Massachusetts 02193

Cover artwork and chapter frontises by Lissa Barnum
Illustrations by Helen Grunstein
Book design by Becky Allen Mixter

Library of Congress Cataloging-in-Publication Data
Mendelsohn, Lotte.
Healthy Mexican regional cookery : a culinary travelogue /
Lotte Mendelsohn.
p.   cm.
Includes bibliographical references and index.
ISBN 1-883280-06-0
1. Cookery, Mexican.   2. Mexico--Description and travel.
I. Title.
TX716.M4M45   1995   95-9409
641.5972--dc20   CIP

First Printing 1995
Printed in the United States of America

1 2 3 4 5 6 7 8 9 10

To a joy unexpected,
belovéd granddaughter

CAYENNE AUGUSTA BARNUM

ABRAZOTES

TO

Bert Mendelsohn, husband, best friend, advisor, grammarian, proofreader, battery, and brake.

Carl, Jeremy, Lissa, Andrew, and Aliza, whose passion for the Mexican table fills every page of this book.

Helen and Max Grunstein, who really started it all—
and whose love, friendship, fair and foul weather steadfastness, and *sobremesas* are what Mexico is all about.

AND

Ilene Horowitz and Sam Schlosberg, more than publishers, enthusiastic friends in food.

Steven Raichlen, whose warmth, energy, and extraordinary craft are a delicious, culinary roadmap for all lovers of food.

Jeff Smith, Craig Wollam, and Chris Schlesinger, for support and the contagious chef's spirit of the "little engine that could!" How do you do it, guys?

Lora Brody, delightful and dauntless, an example for all of us who labor at the feet of the two Gods, "Wonder Kitchen Gadgets" and "Spellcheck."

Diana Kennedy, the Grande Dame of Mexican Cuisine, for a template too perfect to follow, but which inspired even while nudging me in another direction.

Rick and Deanne Bayliss for the wonderful book, *Authentic Mexican,* which has been my cooking guide, when memory and taste buds tired or failed.

Mark Miller, for scholariness and "style."

Heidi Yorkshire, whose professionalism, wit, and friendship helped make a writer out of me.

Karen Sperling, who tried but couldn't—with C.C., who wouldn't!

Maruja and Fernando Barbachano for epitomizing the *amistad* of the Yucatán.

AND FINALLY AND ESPECIALLY TO

George and Penny Jeffers, Rubén Cerdá, family and staff; Jackie Lynott,
Naomi Siegmann, Sally Ayala, Nanette and Emerich Saltzberger,
Bob and Marie Handler, Alistair and Widad MacKenzie,

and all other dear friends in Mexico with whom we shared
so many merry meals.

ART and DESIGN

Lissa Mendelsohn Barnum
(Cover and chapter frontispieces)

Half of the successful graphic design firm of A & L Barnum, Lissa was
born and raised in Mexico City of American parents. She presently resides in
Sydney, Australia, where she works as a designer, illustrator, and painter,
with her husband, Andrew, who is an artist, poet, and musician. The couple
have one daughter, Cayenne Augusta.

Passionately dedicated to the indigenous roots of both Mexico and Australia, Lissa's paintings, self-categorized as "Aus-Mex," are shown in galleries
of naif art in the United States and abroad.

Helen Grunstein
(How-to's and interior support sketches)

Born in Philadelphia, where she received her initial art education at the
School of Industrial Art of the Philadelphia Museum of Art. Before World
War II, she married and moved to Mexico, her husband's homeland. She
continued her art education at Mexico City's *Escuela de Arte le Esmeralda*
and later, individually with several of Mexico's greatest artists. She has since
raised a family and continued her art career (painting, sculpting, and illustrating). The artist has been a dynamic force in the evolution of contemporary art in Mexico, both as an artist and collector. She resides with her husband
in the Mexican capital.

THE
REPUBLIC
OF
MEXICO

TABLE

OF

CONTENTS

LISTA DE RECETAS

Recipe List

PREFACE

Ten years in the information gathering stage and another two in the actual writing, this book has evolved constantly under my fingers. So long glued to the screen of my computer, I realized that the book was contemporizing itself on a parallel with actual life in Mexico. Destinations are changing, and above all, eating habits have changed and continue to do so.

To keep up with this metamorphosis, I simplified recipe techniques and made changes in ingredients—I want everyone to be able to find the raw materials and feel comfortable preparing these delicious dishes. In addition, I paid continuing attention to the latest nutrition findings. In all of these recipes I have *lowered* the fat content drastically. Lard, a prime ingredient in authentic Mexican fare, has without exception been banished and vegetable oils substituted. Does the taste suffer—surprisingly not! The exquisite pungency of most of the cuisine actually benefits from my bit of "healthy" *readjusting*, allowing the complex flavors a brighter spotlight without the distraction of pervasive animal fats.

UNDERSTANDING THE REGIONAL
CUISINES OF MEXICO

Anyone who writes about the "real" Mexico faces a screen of conflicting images. Passion and paganism march unselfconsciously in step with a deep sense of religious commitment. Laughter trades places with tears in a wink; emotions simmer invisibly, ready to erupt seemingly without reason . . . and we may even imagine a Zorro-like script with the swashbuckling drawing of a blade. Romance and danger are omnipresent spices!

As a thirty year resident of Mexico, the food editor of the *Mexico City News* and a long time news and features broadcaster on the CBS affiliate in the Mexican capital, I had a VIP seat for the spectacular adolescence of the complex Hispanic country to our south. It now seems fortunate that I was disinterested in the quicksand-like politics and economics of emerging nations, and instead immersed myself in Mexico's vast treasury of art and handcrafts. Foremost among her crafts are her culinary triumphs. Little known to many aficionados of Mexican food is the wealth of regional cooking to be found all over the Republic. While we travel together I'll try to give you a capsulized taste of the differences the geography and the varying mestizo cultural mixes make in the development of each area's tables.

This book highlights the many facets of travel and available cuisine, of the huge question mark that lies to the south of the United States . . . to document with a smile some of my most memorable moments as her guest . . . and to banish forever the myth that all Mexican food is **hot** and that there is definitely life beyond tacos!

You'll find in these pages a series of "Chismes." To "chismear" in Spanish means to gossip, to exchange experiences. The "Chismes" herein are offered to allow you an insight into what Mexico is truly like for the visitor, no matter how extended the stay.

For over three decades, the days, weeks, and years were marked by celebrations, religious and ethnic, many of them manufactured for the sheer Latin joy to "party," but all of them punctuated by groaning boards of exquisite food and drink. This then, is a "tasting" of those years. Please join me. Your passport?—All you need to cross the border is your sense of humor, your glass, and your napkin—you'll use them all!

Salud y buen provecho!

THE HISTORY OF MEXICAN CUISINE

I'll wager that not one reader in a hundred can name the "big Four" of ethnic cookery in the proper order of "wealth of recipes" inventory. Amando Farga, the Spanish[1] culinary historian, author of *History of Food in Mexico* (*Historia de la Comida en Mexico*), lists them as follows: China, Spain (the influence from the seafaring conquerors) **Mexico,** and Italy. France shuffles along in fifth place. If this is the case, why is so little information available to the culinary interested? Let's explore the phenomenon.

In any bookstore in the United States, **food**, the single subject which is accessible and interesting to everyone, occupies whole sections—its history, economic and political influences, and, of course, endless shelves dedicated to its preparation—cookbooks are an American passion!

Conversely, in a Mexican bookstore, of which there are many, departments dealing with the subject of "culture," stock magazines and books dealing with antique furniture and decor, splendid, coffee-table editions of art books, and complete sections on music. The performing and visual arts are also impressively represented.

Strange then that the most common cultural bond of the earth's peoples, from ancient times to today's bustling world—**food**!—what the Mexican has put in his belly and on his table, is strangely ignored by historians and the serious literary community of the country. Less than a dozen books have been published in Mexico on the subject.

Food is not only a cultural imperative, it is a cultural comparative for most civilized folk, and don't underestimate the food sophistication of our neighbors to the south. Historically they predate the North Americans. Their degree of early, civilization shames us in the areas of medicine, law, and government.

The Toltecs, Zapotecs, and Aztecs perfected whole schools of architecture, feather, gold and silver metal work, frontal lobotomies, and root canal. They also ate magnificently.

Twelve thousand years before Christ the "Man of Tepexpan" lived. His fossilized skeleton, along with bones of the mighty mammoth and the remains of primitive carving tools, were unearthed by anthropologists near the Pyramids of Teotihuácan.

---

[1] Lest you think our Spanish chronicler Farga prejudiced, please let me correct the infamous generalized use of the national adjective, "Spanish." Spanish refers to a language and also to that which comes from Spain. Latin American dishes are correctly described by the name of the country from which they originate—hence a cuisine is: Peruvian, Guatemalan, or in the case of this book, Mexican. To call a typically Mexican dish, Spanish, is to invite a well-aimed concussion with an iron skillet!

These early inhabitants of what is now a suburb of Mexico City, saw the extinction of the huge, land animals, and the gradual shrinking of the Polar ice cap. Indigenous Mexican forbears saw new land masses formed and the most adventurous began the multi-generational migration to the Pacific Coastal areas, to fish and hunt.

It is theorized that wild bands of hunters migrated form Siberia, through Alaska and filtered down the West coast of the continent, arriving at last in Mexico via the Eastern and Western peripheries of the Sierra Madres. To these nomads, agriculture was unknown; meat was their primary sustenance.

A millenium later, new invaders, equally barbaric, came—the Nahoas. Finally, in their wake, families peaceful by nature, little by little established a form of "colony," and farming and fishing became important sources of their daily diet. The receding of the great water masses occurred and what we know of today as the American continent was geologically defined.

Anthropologists and ethnologists feel that the "Mother civilization" to our south, was probably the "Olmeca." The occasional "moon-faced," almond-eyed Mexican that you will today encounter in the center of my beloved ex-home, is a descendent of these ancient adventurers. These early communities not only gathered wild plants and herbs, but also discovered and nurtured a wild grain, hitherto unknown to the world—corn! This mountain grain called today, "cimarron," was about a foot high, and had a flower-like, loose kernel. Little did they dream that they were cultivating one of the plants which would someday divide and define the world into the "wheat, rice, and corn cultures."

The first of the lands' agriculture cycles developed between 10,000 B.C. and 6,000 B.C. Again, in another fossil finding, this time to the west of Mexico City, clues offered by the Coxcatlán Man, establish that by 6,000 B.C. several different kinds of chilis were being cultivated; also squash, beets, and goosefoot herbs (*chenopodium*). Found too, was evidence of a system of crop fertilization using ashes and excrement, and the application of rotating crops by planting a variety of beans or legumes around the periphery of the corn stands, to strengthen and improve their yield.

The aforementioned Amando Farga is of the school of historians who believe in the bridge of Atlantis; the pathway which was trod by the policultural peoples who surrounded the Tropic of Cancer: Moors, Eqyptians, Jews, Indians, and Chinese. He claims the original "Mestizaje" (mixed blood), as the product of these peregrinations. Coming to the point of our research, his theory would indeed be a verification for the diverse influences which have formed the vast inventory of over 2,000 regional recipes—so little known outside the country's borders.

Continuing south and east, the original Mayans were a supposed mystical-mixture of these cultures. This helps to explain their glyphs and stellae, as well as their dominance of astronomy, mathematics, and a supremely com-plicated language and alphabet which is still largely a mystery.

Unfortunately, with all their sophistication and knowledge, class-consciousness and class-behavior differences, caused the downfall of the Mayan civilization. Both chaotic political struggles and bloody machinations for power among the priesthood and the aristocracy, brought about the end of the glory that was Mayaland, just a few years into the 15th century.

Later, in the same century, Columbus was hoisting sail. His passion and Queen Isabella's eye for profit sent our discoverer westward in search of the riches of the spice trade! His first voyages, and later Cortes' historic foray, brought many of our common kitchen cupboard ingredients to the attention of the Spanish, and later, other European Courts; garlic, caraway, poppy seeds, basil, anise, cloves, and cumin. The list is long, but many are less known and appreciated. *Epazote*, known in the United States as the weed "wormseed," gives flavor to most fine pork dishes and "sarsparilla," which became our grandmothers' favorite soda-fountain flavor.

Our last contributing piece of data is also quite pertinent. There are over 170 different, indigigenous languages and dialects spoken in Mexico today; a vital factor in the difficult task of educating and unifying this race, which British author John Lincoln has described so well with th single adjective, "prickly." It also explains the paucity of information about much of Mexico, and in particular, her regional cuisine. From all of this variegated "aculturalization" come the mentioned, two thousand dishes.

While it may appear that I've strayed from the subject of food as a cultural form, it's impossible to grasp the breadth of the influences on the subject without some historical insight. All of these elements are factors in the development of Mexico's table today.

Understand that tacos and enchiladas are her "fast foods," as omnipresent and irresistible, as our "hot dogs" and fries. However, if the definition of "gourmet" means unusual, exciting, and painstakingly prepared, then gourmet fare can be found in the humblest of Mexico's street cafés as wll as the most elegant mansions of her cities.

It is a thoroughly "Mestizo" art form, embodying centuries of culinary cross-pollenization, utilization of the land's bounty, and the strong sense of individuality that is so deeply Mexican.

THE MEXICANIZATION OF A PANTRY

"Oh, this recipe sounds so good!" . . . and I'm off like a top, spinning around between my garage freezer and kitchen pantry, digging into the back of the cabinets (. . . greasy shelves! . . . I must get in here and dust and change the shelf lining and . . . later!) . . . like a terrier after a mouse. Memory tells me that I have that can of Jalapeños here someplace, but the actual inventory shakes its head "no" at the grey cells. I distinctly remember seeing it when I was looking for something to jazz up the boys' peanut butter sandwiches—an electrifying combination for all lovers of things fiery!

This is the time to re-evaluate your kitchen inventory, to turn over a new leaf or leaves . . . avocado, coriander, banana foliage, etc. are all used to flavor advantage in Latin American kitchens, and now corn husks and banana leaves are available in many markets. Ready—I'm going to "Mexicanize" your cupboards.

Keep all your ethnic food supplies in one place. It makes grocery lists simpler to formulate and shopping just that much easier.

Following is a modest, basic inventory to start you on your way. Remember to replace spices often, they lose their pungency with time. Also, store them in a cool, dark place—it extends their life.

SPICES

Annato seeds (*achiote*) to be ground in a spice mill
Cinnamon sticks (*canla en raja*)
Cloves, whole (*clavos enteros*)
Coriander (*cilantro*) leaves, not seeds (Durkee)
Cumin, ground (*comino molido*)
Sesame seeds (*ajonjolí*)

VARIOUS

White rice (Goya, Valencia, or Uncle Ben)
Quick Grits (Quaker)
Corn "Masa Harina" (Quaker) and "Masa Rica" (Goya)—
    see sources
Canned tomatillos (*tomate verde*) (Goya and Herdez)
Canned Cuítlacoche or Huítlacoche (*Clemente Jacques*)
Green sauce (La Victoria TacoSauce)
Canned black beans

Dried beans black, red, and golden
Dried chilies, mulato, ancho, pasilla
Canned chipotle chilies (various brands, I like San Marcos)
Canned Jalapeños (buy the slices if you can)
Red hot sauce (McIlhenny's Tabasco is the only one I use)
Green hot sauce (Tabasco Jalapeño Sauce, La Victoria)
Maggi liquid seasoning (used as a flavor enhancer for
         everything)
Bouillon cubes, chicken and beef (Maggi or Herb Ox)

LIST OF SOURCES

Coyote Cafe General Store: Sante Fe, NM: Dried and fresh chilies, Mexican herbs and spices, etc. Catalogue: 505-982-2454.

Dean & Deluca: NY, NY. Ethnic and tropical produce and most anything else you need. 212-431-1691.

Frieda's, Inc.: (Look for the purple stickers.) Originally wholesale only, now available in supermarkets and specialty stores. For an overall sampling of the dried chilies used in this book's recipes, ask for the "Dried Chile Shipper." Frieda's also stocks fresh chilies and tropical fruits. Catalogue: 1-800-241-1771.

King Arthur Flour Baker's Catalogue: White, yellow, and blue cornmeal (the best), diced dried fruits, spice grinders, high quality kitchen gadgets. 1-800-777-4434.

Tabasco Country Store: Tabasco sauce, Jalapeño sauce, bottled, dry seasonings, chili-themed novelties, and unique serving ware for salsa, tortillas, and other specialties. Catalogue: 1-800-634-9599.

Williams Sonoma: Electric tortilla press, tortilla warmers, ceramic servers, salsa, bean dips, and no-fat chips.
Catalogue: 1-800-541-2233.

Felicidades! Now you're ready for the great bi-culturalization
of your cookery.

HOW TO SHOP
IN A
MEXICAN MARKET

El Regato
(ray-got-ay´-oh)

One of the most common clichés about travel is that it "broadens one." In the case of shopping in Mexico, the broadening often goes against every rule of good manners Mama ever taught us. Bargaining or *regateo*, as it's called in Spanish, is not optional, it's mandatory!

Take heart however, you timorous shoppers, you are **not** taking unfair advantage of a desparate populous. You're indulging in the great national sport; a game as passionately played and enjoyed as soccer or jai alai—Mexicans love to haggle!

Like any sport, there are a few basic rules. But again like athletics, a great deal of skill, creativity, body language, and theatrics are also in play. Let me inivite you to join me in a classic transaction *a la Mexicana*.

The Setting: The basket stand in an urban, public market.

The Players: Juan (or Juana) the vendor. You alone, or with companion(s).

The Game: Saunter through the area, and pass the stand with a blank (or if acting is your thing, a Noel Coward-like expression of total *boredom*). If your peripheral vision is good, **scan the inventory** and take note of your choice. Do not make eye contact with Juan.

Juan: *Buenos Días Señor(a)(es). Qué se antoja?* or *"Qué le gusta"* (What tempts you? What do you like?)

Step 1: Smile slightly and nod your head in a non-commital, slightly negative way. *Nada* (nah-dah), *gracias.* This gives you the opportunity to scope out the stand up close.

Juan: *Ay Señores* . . . here follows an ingratiating first plea usually extolling the virtues of the merchandise in general, often accompanied by the offering to smell, touch, drape around, or whatever, the object for sale.

Step 2: Stand still, look pleasant, and let him (her) pitch . . . you will find that Juan's pitch is longer and more passionate than Juana's, I've never understood why, but men seem to "get into" the sport with more enthusiasm.

Now, slowly **reach for something totally different** from what you actually have interest in, and examine it. **Return it** to its place or to the "sales associate." **Shrug your shoulders**, (indifference is the key here), and walk away.

Step 3: Tour the rest of the market (if there are several things you want to buy, you can choreograph your rounds so that you repeat this scenario several times, eating up the waiting time for step four. You're also getting better at this, and beginning to have fun.

Step 4: (This is your big scene.) **Stroll by the basket stand again.** Juan will recognise you have no fear, and **hesitate** again. **Pick up something** (remember, not the item you covet), and **converse with your companion**. (Be aware that the wily vendor understands everything you say, either because of having heard it a jillion times before, or because Mexican marketers are omniscient when it comes to foreign "fair game.") **Talk nicely** about the better quality of the goods at another stand, for example: *I think the handles were stronger and better made at the other stand, don't you,—but I like the design of this one—oh, I don't know, it's so hard to tell the difference, but the other was much cheaper*—**wrinkle your brow and sigh**, *Cuánto es?* (*How much is it?*) Now, adjust your greasepaint, **let your lower jaw drop and look** incredulous. **Hand back the item** as if it contained Cleopatra's asp, and **give a little chuckle** to indicate to him that you both know he was joking.

Step 5: Offer half. When you've **"halved" several times** back and forth, turn your attention to the item you really want and with a deprecatory shrug **ask**—*y esto?* (*And this one?*) Now, you're finally ready to bargain for your treasure. **Repeat steps 1 through 4.**

Step 6. (This is your second big chance at stardom.) **Look, very, very stern** and exasperated, **waggle your erect index finger** energetically from left to right, and **WALK AWAY.** (Please note: Once in a while your canny opponent will sulk and not play anymore, but **usually**, he'll counter in a shout aimed at your disappearing back.) **Return**, all gracious delight and thanks, **pay** for your booty, and control your **chortle** of triumph until you're out of sight.

(Note: A bit of insider trivia for street or market shopping. Shop early in the morning, as soon as they are set up for business. Mexicans consider the first sale a blesséd omen for a prosperous day, and the bargaining is easiest if they have not yet made that first peso. When you pay for your purchase, the vendor will kiss the bill, cross him or herself with it, and then tuck it away with a smile and a sigh of satisfaction.)

A variation on the bargaining theme is done in fine stores also, particularly in jewelry shops. I've even learned to do this in the good old US of A, and you'd be surprised at the upscale establishments that will go along with the request.

This is how it goes. *Yes, I'm considering— it's really quite handsome. What's the price **with** my discount?* Shrug slightly—*Is that the best you can do? Well, thank you—oh, and if I pay cash rather than use a credit card, how much larger will the discount be?* Once the price is settled, remember that Mexicans are always polite. *Thank you, it's truly been a pleasure doing business with you—oh, and could I have one of those nice little chamois bags to put it in?—and I'd like to have several business cards so that I can send my friends!*

Your first market purchase may exhaust you and cause a momentary pang of bad conscience (—*but the asking price is so **cheap**!*"). Repeat after me, *this is fun and sport for Juanito,* a bit like retail "chess"—don't deprive him of a good match. Cherish the rush of adrenaline which comes with a good buy fairly consummated, and always keep in mind, in Mexico *regateo* is an art form!

BAJA
CALIFORNIA

BAJA CALIFORNIA

Quintana Roo and *Baja California* are diametrically opposite each other on a map of the Republic of Mexico, but the two extremes have much in common—recent discovery and exploitation by the international world of hoteliers, and adoption by the burgeoning jet set! Unfortunately neither of these innovations is a plus. But let me concentrate here on Baja.

Baja California is an arid, sparsely settled, 800 mile-long peninsula. There is a moonscape quality about much of its sandy expanse, broken only by the visually welcome undulations of the Sierra San Pedro Mártir. *Baja*, divided into two almost equal halves, the south half of which is called logically *Baja California Sur*, was an escapist's Eden.

Unfortunately, there is an increasing explosion of unplanned commerce popping up to mar this paradise. The results: vast, featureless trailer parks; littering with a frightening disregard for the ecology; proliferation of ugly fast service "joints;" price gouging and the increasing, defensive rudeness of a normally polite people.

Nonetheless, there is still spectacular sportfishing, whale watching, surfing, and dune buggy jaunts for the outdoorsmen, "snowbirds," and the hip youth with their surf boards poked out the windows of rocking RV's cruising the Trans Peninsular highway.

For the tourist seeking action and super, modern plumbing facilities, keep heading for La Paz and then on to whale watchers' heaven, Los Cabos. Hotels for the discriminating include: Hotel La Posada, Cabañas de Los Arcos, and Los Arcos Hotel in La Paz; the Twin Dolphin and the Palmilla in San José del Cabo, and in Cabo San Lucas (bring money), when feeling plush, we like the Solmar and the Clarion.

THINGS TO SEE, DO, and EAT

Tijuana: Elegant shopping on Avenida Revolución or off-price shopping generally on the second floor of an unlikely looking building or in someone's garage. Remember, this is a duty-free zone, so if you're diligent and make friends with your cab driver, you may hit shopper's pay dirt! Don't miss the **Bol Corona**, an ex-bowling alley turned funky restaurant with memorable *burritos*.

On the way to Ensenada: (Km 59. La Misión exit) Stop at the charming and filling **La Fonda Restaurant Bar**. Order the triple entrée special and the lemon pie.

Ensenada: Another shopper's mecca with good buys in leather. For truly unusual gold and silver jewelry, don't miss **Artes Bitterlin** and **La Mina de Salomón**.

For a true taste of the Mexican fishing industry, hit the pungent morning fish market *(Mercado de Pesca)*. Enjoy a myriad of little seafood places specializing in abalone and "lobster"—it's really crayfish, but order it in *Mojo de Ajo* (garlic butter) and you may never leave. "Eggs a la Claudia" at the—feels like an aquarium—**Restaurant del Mar**. For wine lovers the **Bodegas de Santo Tomás** offers a tour and tastings. (So-so quality but improving—try the red.) Have a cocktail at the town's cultural center, once a gambling casino. The octagonal Riviera del Pacífico boasts ceilings painted with Pompeiian-like murals of bacchanals, and if you close your eyes, you can imagine the ghosts of the high rollers from Hollywood who once gambled there.

Cataviña: A haven for cactus lovers. Several species, some exclusive to Baja *(cirios,* elephant cactus) grow in abundance here—nothing else.

Santa Rosalía: Circled by an odd seismic ring of inverted cones, the scars of past strip mining accentuate the Star Wars feeling of the town. Another oddity is the iron church, designed by the famed Mr. Eiffel for the Paris Worlds' Fair (1898) and brought to Baja in pieces and reassembled.

PÓMPANO EN MOJO DE AJO

Pompano in Garlic Oil

Serves 4

1 head garlic, peeled and sliced
¼ cup olive oil
2 pounds Pompano, sea bass, or
    flatfish, whole
salt and pepper, to taste
juice of 1 orange
juice of 1 lemon
2 tablespoons parsley, minced

This is definitely not a dish to be enjoyed right before a board meeting in a small room, but my oh my, how delicious it is! Although I've assigned the recipe to Baja California, the fisherman's paradise, it can be ordered and prepared from the north to the south with whatever white-fleshed fish has been brought in on your shopping day.

1. Mince 1 garlic clove and soak the remaining sliced cloves in the olive oil while you clean the fish.
2. Pat the fish dry and rub with the minced clove of garlic. Sprinkle with salt and pepper and bake in a 350°F oven for 45 minutes, basting with the juice of the orange.
3. Heat the oil and sauté the rest of the garlic slices very slowly—"stay with it" and allow them to turn just golden. Remove the garlic cloves and add the lemon juice, salt, pepper, and minced parsley. Serve the hot sauce on the fish.

PAN DE SANTA ROSALÍA

Santa Rosalía is an anomoly. A dusty city, visually Gallic, but with a climate from the deepest reaches of Hell. The few winter days when it is habitable, it plays host to yachtsmen and sport fishermen. This former copper mining town is the unlikely home of a steel church designed buy A.E. Eiffel of Parisian tower fame, financed by German capital, and built by the slave labor of the local Seri Indians.

Pan de Santa Rosalía is a French bread made from the dough for the famed "baguette" and now appearing in every bread shop in the Republic either as *bolillos* or *teleras*. *Bolillos* are eaten in myriad ways, while the flat, tri-scored *telera*, is usually the crusty base for a "torta," the Mexican version of our sandwich.

SOPA DE ALMEJAS

Clam Soup

Serves 6

2 tablespoons olive oil
1 large onion, chopped
2 cups chopped celery
2 cloves garlic, minced
3 cups potatoes, peeled and
    cubed
8 cups clam juice (bottled will
    do very well)
salt and pepper, to taste
2 cups fresh clams, coarsely
    chopped and drained
1½ cups finely chopped
    parsley
juice of 1 lime
splash of Maggi and Tabasco

Food is not Baja California's strong point, but what can be bad about a soup that reminds you of Italian white clam sauce? I think this recipe closely approximates the version found in almost any beachside bistro on the peninsula.

Note: *If you are a true mollusk lover, be sure to ask for "chocolate clams." They are so named because of the color of their shells, and the Bajans always eat them raw with a squirt of lime juice and a splash each of Maggi and Tabasco sauce.*

1. Heat 1 tablespoon of the oil in a large pot or Dutch oven, add the onion, celery, and garlic and cook until transparent.
2. Add the potatoes, bottled or fresh clam juice and simmer, covered, over low heat, for 15 minutes or until the potatoes are tender. Add salt and pepper to taste.
3. Ten minutes before serving, bring the broth to a boil, add any clam juice from the fresh clams and chopped clams themselves. Return just to a simmer (overcooking renders the clams rubbery), and add the chopped parsley, remaining olive oil, lime juice, Maggi, and Tabasco. Serve immediately.

GUACAMOLE "LEGÍTIMO"

Honest-to-God Guacamole

Yield: Dip for 6

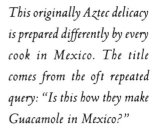

This originally *Aztec* delicacy is prepared differently by every cook in Mexico. The title comes from the oft repeated query: "Is this how they make Guacamole in Mexico?"

Because America has so enthusiastically adopted the creamy verdancy of this dish, and Baja California is so American in so many ways, I'll attribute this version to the sandy reaches of B.C.

3 large, ripe avocados
1 tablespoon lemon or lime juice
¼ cup onion, grated
1 medium tomato, peeled, seeds removed, and chopped
2 tablespoons sour cream (optional)
1 Jalapeño pepper,[1] seeded, deveined, and chopped fine (use gloves)
fresh coriander/cilantro, to taste, chopped
salt, to taste

Optional Additions:
⅓ cup cheese, Feta or farmer's, finely crumbled
2 slices bacon, fried crisp and finely crumbled
substitute mayonnaise or 2 tablespoons olive oil for the sour cream

1. Peel and mash the avocados. Add the lemon juice, onion, and tomato.
2. Stir in the sour cream, Jalapeño, and coriander/cilantro. Add more Jalapeño pepper here and the optional cheese and bacon. Taste and add salt if desired.
3. If you make ahead of serving time, place the avocado pit in the guacamole[2] and cover with plastic wrap directly on the surface of the dip. Serve with hot tortilla chips.

---

[1] 1 teaspoon Jalapeño sauce (I use McIlhenny's) can be substituted.
[2] The pit keeps the mixture from turning brown.

HERBS AND SPICES

E-specially E-spicy

Speaking a foreign language without an accent is no mean feat!

Anglos seem to be congenitally unable to roll their "r"s and the Mexicans have difficulty beginning a word with the "s" sound. Results: we might say "pero" (which means "but") when we are referring to the dog (perro), and the Mexicano would say "this e-spaghetti is not e-spicy enough"—So much for recalcitrant tongues!

Because of the many influences merging on the Mexican tables, a wealth of common herbs are used; parsley, garlic, bay leaves, oregano, and even mint, but there are also three very distinctive greens that flavor the regional dishes:

- Coriander or cilantro *(coriandrum sativum)* used to be an exotic, but it is now almost as popular as parsley.

- Epazote *(chenopodium abrosioides)* wormseed or pigweed.

- Hoja Santa or Hierba Santa *(piper sanctum)*.

The spices include cinnamon *(canela)*, cloves *(clavo de olor)*, black pepper *(pimienta negra)*, cumin *(comino)*, and annato *(achiote)*.

BURRITO DE MACHACA DE MANTARAYA

. . . .

Dried Skate Burrito

Serves 4

½ pound skate jerky
juice of 2 large lemons
⅓ cup vegetable oil
1 medium onion, minced
2 cloves garlic, peeled and
    mashed
3 canned chipotle chilies,
    drained, seeds removed
3 ripe plum tomatoes,
    chopped fine and drained
salt, to taste
8 large-size flour tortillas

This is a Baja California specialty enjoyed in every small community on the Pacific coast of Baja. It is normally made with Poblano chilies, but this version is one we discovered in agricultural San Quintín. Perhaps it was so savory because the tomatoes used were still warm from the fields.

Follow the recipe for Cecina *(jerky) on page 51 substituting cleaned skate wings for the beef and following the instructions starting with step 2.*

1. On a baking sheet, lay out the skate jerky, sprinkle with lemon juice, and toast under the broiler until crispy. When cool, shred.
2. In a medium-sized skillet, heat the oil and sauté the onion and garlic. Lower the heat to medium and add the jerky. Stir until the mixture begins to crisp, about 8 minutes.
3. Shred the chipotles with 2 forks and add with the tomatoes to the jerky mixture. Cook over low flame for 5 minutes to allow the flavors to blend. Add salt if necessary.
4. Spoon into heated tortillas, roll, and fold the ends, and serve at once on a heated platter.

FRIJOLES REFRITOS

Their omnipresence on menus south of the Border and on the Border, detracts not at all from their enjoyment, every day, everywhere in Mexico.

Refried Beans

Serves 6

1 cup beans (red kidney or black)
1 tablespoon olive oil
1 medium onion, minced
1 clove garlic, peeled and mashed
salt, to taste
tortilla chips (nachos)
grated cheese

1. Soak the beans overnight in cold water to cover.
2. Cook the beans in 1 quart of water, covered, until tender, about 1½ hours. Be sure to skim off any foam that rises to the top. Drain.
3. Heat the olive oil in a medium-sized skillet. Sauté the onion and garlic until transparent. Add the beans and fry over low heat for about 10 minutes, mashing the beans and blending with the onion and garlic. The beans should be almost dry but crisping on the outside. Salt to taste.
4. Turn out onto a heated platter in the form of a small meatloaf. Stud with tortilla chips and sprinkle with grated cheese.

TACOS PIONERO

Pioneer's Tacos

Serves 4

> Mexico's savory answer to our bacon cheeseburger can be ordered in the many spotless Sanborn's restaurants to be found all over the Republic. Served with fresh Salsa Mexicana (page 168), you may never call for the catsup bottle again.

½ pound skirt steak, cut into
    12 strips
vegetable oil
12 flour tortillas
8 strips of bacon, cooked just
    until crisp and drained
4 slices of baked ham, cut into 16 strips
1 large onion, sliced thin
4 slices of white Cheddar cheese
4 sprigs of curly parsley
fresh *Salsa Mexicana* (see page 168)

1. Quick-fry or grill the steak strips in a small amount of vegetable oil.
2. In the center of each of 4 heated tortillas, pile 2 strips of bacon, 4 slices of ham, and several onion slices on top of 1 slice of cheese. Roll and brown on all sides in an oiled skillet.
3. On each of 4 heated plates, cut 1 filled taco into thirds, and serve with 2 more heated tortillas tucked under each. Garnish with parsley and serve with *Salsa Mexicana* on the side.

POSTRE REAL DE CAFÉ

Coffee Dessert

Serves 4

Because the tip of Baja is so far from everything, deliveries of fresh food are often erratic. In every cook's pantry there are cans of condensed and evaporated milk, vanilla cookies (Marías) and of course the ubiquitous instant coffee. This quick dessert is a Mexican favorite.

20 *María* (Arrowroot-type) wafers
4 teaspoons instant coffee
tiny pinch of salt
3 tablespoons brandy
1 can condensed milk
½ cup corn syrup

1. Pulverize the wafers. (I break them up in a plastic bag first and then give them a quick whirr in the blender.)
2. To the blender, add the instant coffee, salt, and brandy. Blend until the coffee is dissolved. Add the condensed milk and corn syrup. Blend thoroughly and pour into parfait or custard cups. Serve topped with sweetened whipped cream and a few granules of instant coffee for color.

"RED BONES AND GARLIC"

There's an idiomatic phrase in Spanish which connotes the purest, most profound type of nationalism; to wit: *Es Mexicano de hueso colorado*. In English, this would be compared to, "Red-Blooded American," but in Spanish it comes up "Red-Boned."

My blond, blue-eyed daughter, Lissa Mendelsohn Barnum, born, bred, and "culturalized" in Mexico, is a "red-boned" Mexican food fanatic!

I suppose it all started when a Brazilian friend of mine sympathetically "tsk-tsked" when I complained about my first son's lack of appetite

"What are you feeding him?," she asked. When I reeled off the sterile delicacies from the little jars imported from the U.S., she made a face, opened a jar and forced a teaspoon of a beige "something," down my throat . . . ecch!!!! . . . Not only tasteless, but truly unidentifiable. . . . All the baby food, in all of the jars tasted the same. . . . Only the colors changed.

"Yecch?" she said, "That's exactly the way he feels!"

Thus started the transition from breast milk to haute cuisine in the blender, when feeding my brood.

The kids savored everything from Boeuf Bourguignonne to Pasta Puttanesca, all whizzed to digestible consistency in Mr. Oster's wonderful invention. . . . Aside from developing gourmet palates, they were different in other ways too.

Daddy returned home early one evening and found me with my golden haired baby daughter, nestled against my shoulder after a feeding. He nuzzled the nape of her neck and drew away with a grin, remarking wryly, "Everyone else's kids smell of Johnson's Baby Powder, ours always smell of garlic!"

By primary school age, it became apparent that our youngest child was different from her brothers when it came to eating habits. . . . She seemed to exist on air. . . . She didn't come to the table hungry, regardless of the menu. . . . It appeared as though we'd given birth to a human bromeliad! Furthering the mystery, she was never sick, didn't look pale or wan. She was an active, wiry elf. Just where did the energy and graceful growth come from? It was a long, unsolved question.

Several years ago, while visiting her in Australia, I opened her refrigerator door and there, in neat alignment, with milk, fresh vegetables, and cheeses, sat fourteen jars of Jalapeño peppers. At that time, in Sydney, the only chilies available came in 5 kilo commercial-sized cans. Once the can was opened, the peppers had to be transferred to glass jars to keep them from fermenting and spoiling. . . . Why this excess inventory?

"I have a Jalapeño with every meal, otherwise everything tastes bland!" And then, the provenance of this passion unfolded.

"Do you remember when you thought I wasn't eating? Don't worry, I ate. I ate with the *muchachas* in the kitchen. I loved their hot foods. Theirs was much more interesting, much more satisfying than what you "guys" ate. . . . Mum, cook and the other girls were afraid to tell you and so was I. . . . Would you have really allowed me to eat all those wonderful fried-in-lard offal dishes, along with beans and rice every day; plus that heavenly incendiary stuff?"

Her conspiratorial grin invited a truthful response. . . . "Definitely not!," I answered.

Is the palate for true Mexican food acquired? If my three gourmands are any indication, the answer is a resounding YES!!! But, the acquisition should start early.

I wonder if the cook threw a chili into the baby food blender when my back was turned. . . . It wouldn't surprise me at all!

EL NORTE

States of:

CHIHUAHUA,
COAHUILA,
NUEVO LEÓN,
SONORA,
ZACATECAS,
DURANGO

THE NORTH

The northern part of Mexico is the area and culture most familiar to North Americans. Geographically, much of it abuts California, New Mexico, and Texas, and both its glories and its tensions are played out in the cultural seesaw of life on the Border. Although the states of Zacatecas and Durango have no common border with the U.S. and lie touching the belly of Central Mexico, their attitudes, ranching life-styles and cuisine have a great deal in common with the border states, and for that reason I include them in this chapter.

El Norte is also well known to aficionados of the cowboy western. The majority of films of this genre have been shot in this high desert country, where both the topography and the pure light are the cinematographers' delight. Single dimension scenery flats, depicting towns from old John Wayne movies, pop up at the strangest times and close to the most desolate towns.

In Ciudad Cuauhtémoc, Chihuahua, groups of tow-headed children are an unlikely part of the scene. Descendants of Mennonites who were sold the land by President Alvaro Obregón in the mid-19th century, the conservative sect prospers through dairy farming. Their creamery products, in particular a salty, feta-like cheese, are sold in grocery stores in the town proper.

The vast ranches of the north mean beef, and the beef from Chihuahua and Coahuila is one of Mexico's greatest prides. It is prepared simply, over braziers, lightly topped with a spicy tomato sauce, coaxed into savory stews, or sun-dried and shredded Vaquero-style (*cecina, machaca*). Similar to our own beef jerky, the dried meat is shredded then tossed with beaten eggs, for a rib-hugging breakfast, or simply basted with oil and lemon juice and served to hungry folk with good teeth!

As cattle country, for the most part, it is dusty and unforgiving, yet parts are widely beautiful. Chihuahua's famous *Cañon del Cobre* (Copper Canyon) railway, wends sinuously over the Sierra Madre Occidental mountains rumbling through eighty odd tunnels and over thirty-six hair raising bridges. The views are unforgettable for those without a tendency to vertigo.

Chihuahua is also Tarahumara country. The Tarahumara Indians live in the most inaccessible mountain reaches and are known for their marathon-running ability. They are ceremonially pitted against the rugged, small horses of the region, whom they easily outrun. Part of the ceremonies (as with the Yáquis of Sonora) involves the ingestion of hallucinatory substances like *peyote*, which induce a trance-like state and the ability to perform almost super-humanly.

Two other culinary facts apply in this vast region: Don't look for corn tortillas. *El Norte*, is the birthplace of the tender, pale, flour tortilla, usually wrapped around the other area staple, beans (*frijoles*). Nowhere in the Republic is there a greater variety of recipes for this Mexican staple. Look in this chapter for several delicious ways to serve and prepare them.

Durango is best known for three things: big, golden scorpions (*alacranes güeros*); marvelous country music, accompanied on a wooden-slatted percussion contraption, which is slung around the neck and attacked with mallets and ferocious energy; and spaghetti-Western movie producers.

Zacatecas is a windy state, unfortunately little visited by the tourist.

For art lovers (of all persuasions, from the classic to the contemporary), the city of Zacatecas boasts a veritable treasure trove of fine art.

Pedro and Rafael Coronel, world-famous artists of the Mexican late 20th century school, have been generous to their native city. The Pedro Coronel Museum is the home of the brother's extensive and eclectic art collection.

In the convent of *Nuestra Señora de Guadalupe* you will find the Museum of Viceregal Art, reported to have one of the most important collections of Colonial art in the world. Also, do not miss the Museo Francisco Goítia.

Saltillo, the capital of the state of Coahuila, has little to recommend it to the visitor seeking beauty. It is largely industrial. What it does have are some fine dining establishments maintained by the heavy business traffic between the *maquiladores* (machine assembly plants) and the Border. It is also the hub for a developing wine growing region, offering the natural vine stress that many winemakers seek.

In the excellent *Cadogan Guide to Mexico* (Katherine & Charlotte Thompson), Monterrey, *Nuevo León* is referred to as "the ugly duckling of Mexico, showing every inclination to turn into a swan." As the third largest city in the Republic, the city owes its phenomenal growth and wealth to large industry and the vision and energy of a few founding families. The hotel and restaurant tariffs are high with little of touristic merit to warrant more than an overnight stay. This is a city dedicated to business and its practitioners on generous expense accounts.

The cuisine of the North is simple and businesslike too. It is also responsible for the erroneous idea among strangers that all of Mexico eats the *Norteño* way. I hope these pages underline the best and invite you to continue south, salivating in anticipation.

THINGS TO SEE, DO, AND EAT

Chihuahua City: The terminal for the famous **Copper Canyon Railway**. Make sure you get first-class accommodations. If none are available, wait for the next train. *Queso de Chihuahua* is a a firm, mild Cheddar-like cheese that is popular throughout the Republic and has its origins here. And this is the country to order beef.

Zacatecas City: The end of August through early September are fiesta days. There is a mock fight between the Moors and the Christians which has color and charm for the photographer (use a telephoto lens and ask permission to snap religious ceremonies). Don't miss the extraordinary **Rafael Coronel** mask collection at the **Convento de San Francisco**.

Things to eat: Chile Poblano (see page 43) sautéed with cheese *(Rajas con Queso)*, pork dishes with several kinds of *mole* (see *Pipián Verde* recipe page 240).

Monterrey: The super macho, **El Tío Restaurant** west of the city, specializes in butter and brandy-injected steaks and spit-roasted kid (*Cabrito al Pastor*). Have a drink in the bar of the **Hotel Ancira**, famous as the hotel into whose lobby Pancho Villa rode his horse. (It makes good retelling back home!) Tour the **Cervecería Cuautémoc**, the largest in the country producing wonderful beer. If you like dark beer, try my favorite, "xxx" Tres Equis.

Hermosillo: This city is known for humungous, white flour tortillas. Try the herbed mushroom tacos (you'll need both hands), at the **Callejoncito** restaurant.

Bahía Kino: This is the home market of the Seri Indians, master sculptors of wildlife. The Seris carve from ironwood, which makes their satiny modeling even more special. Bargain, they expect it!

Guaymas: In the old port city part of Guaymas, "Chato's" is moderately priced and serves whatever the catch of the day may be. Ask for it in *mojo de ajo* (garlic butter).

After a day of superb sportfishing, watch the sunset from San Carlos beach while you nurse a frosty margarita. The **Posada San Carlos** is a good place for fish tacos, the wonderful Pacific red snapper, or your own catch if the chef's in a good mood.

If you're enamored of sea shells as I am, tuck a plastic bag in your purse or pocket and spend a few hours at Los Algodónes beach (about four miles past San Carlos). November to early April are the best months for "conchologists."

MÓCHOMOS CHIHUAHUENSES

Chihuahua Appetizer

Serves 6–8

2 pounds of pork shoulder
1 large onion
3 cloves garlic, peeled
chicken broth
2 tablespoons of bacon fat
  (or vegetable oil)
2 cups of guacamole
  (see page 19)

1. In a heavy saucepan, boil the meat, onion, and garlic with enough broth so that when it is done there is no liquid left.
2. Allow the meat to cool slightly and shred fine.
3. Heat the fat or oil in a large skillet and fry the shredded pork just until damp and crisp.
4. Serve at once, mounded in the center of a round platter, and ladle guacamole sauce around it. Accompany with hot flour or corn tortillas and icy Mexican beer.

This simple, but hearty snack from Chihuahua, can be enjoyed Friday and Saturday evenings, sitting on the pretty square (zócalo) of Aquíles Serdán. It's impossible not to foot tap while watching the frenzied, quick-step gyrations executed to the rowdy, ranchera music.

For a heavier dinner later, go up the hill to El Mesón de Chihuahua el Viejo. The fragrance of their cumin-perfumed tamales will seduce you before you reach the front door.

SOPA DE ZANAHORIAS

Carrot Bisque

Serves 6

4 tablespoons oil
1 medium-sized onion, chopped
8 medium-sized carrots, sliced thin or chopped
2 tablespoons butter or margarine
1 teaspoon salt
3 teaspoons rice or potato flour
½ cup water
1 teaspoon brown sugar
4 tablespoons parsley, finely chopped
4 cups chicken broth, all fat removed
⅛ teaspoon cumin
2 dashes nutmeg
freshly grated black pepper
¼ cup heavy cream (omitted or substitute low-fat ricotta)
parsley sprigs for garnish

The best cook I ever had in Mexico was from Jeréz, Zacatecas. All Mexicans involved in the kitchen make wonderful soup, but Sabina had a special "angel"[1] with carrots. She swore the secret was to choose pointy, tapering carrots—insisting they were sweeter than the stubby kind.

This is not a low-fat soup in its richer version (with the heavy cream), but the flavor is true even with the deletion of the cream or ricotta.

1. In a medium-sized skillet, heat the oil and sauté the onion until transparent. Add the carrots and continue to cook slowly until tender, about 5 minutes. Place into a blender and purée.
2. In a small saucepan, melt 2 tablespoons of butter and blend with the salt, flour, and water, allowing it to brown slightly for flavor. Add the sugar and parsley and blend into the carrot mixture.
3. Heat the broth, add the cumin, nutmeg, and pepper, and stir in the thickened carrot mixture. Allow to simmer for 5 minutes.
4. Stir in heavy cream (or ricotta) and bring to a simmer, (do not allow to boil). Serve garnished with parsley sprigs.

---

[1] To have "angel" means to have luck. I suppose the saying originates from the guardian angel concept.

OSTIONES DE GUAYMAS

....

Oysters, Guaymas-style

Serves 6–8

The Mexicans are as crazy about "Beisbol," as we Americans are. One of the many places in which to watch the Mexican fan let loose his Latin passion for the game is the Del Mar Restaurant in Guaymas. Sit at the bar, watch the mammoth TV screen, and slurp down these heavenly mollusks—they'll make an athlete out of anyone!

4 dozen large fresh oysters
3 tablespoons lemon juice
1½ tablespoons salt
4 onions, chopped fine
½ cup olive oil
1 cup vinegar (any variety)
1 teaspoon allspice
1 teaspoon pepper
6 cloves garlic, broiled and chopped
2 canned Jalepeño chilies, cut into fine strips

1. Shuck the oysters, reserving the shells, and put them in a pot with 1 cup of water, the lemon juice, and 1 tablespoon of salt, and simmer about 5 minutes, or until the edges curl.
2. In a large bowl, soak the onions in 1½ cups of boiling water with 1 teaspoon of salt for 5 minutes. Drain and sauté in hot oil for 2–3 minutes. Add to the oysters. Add the vinegar, allspice, pepper, garlic, chili, and 2 tablespoons of juice from the canned chilies. Cover the bowl and let stand for 24 hours in the refrigerator.
3. Wash the oyster shells well. Serve the cooked oysters in a bowl, with a half shell used as a scooper. Wonderful with hot *bolillos*. (A French baguette or hard roll will do nicely).

MACHACA CON HUEVO

Shredded Beef with Egg

Serves 4

⅓ cup vegetable oil
1 cup tomatoes, chopped fine
1 small onion, chopped fine
2–3 serrano chiles,[1] seeded and
   chopped fine
2 cups dried beef or cecina
   (see page 43), shredded
juice of 1 lime or ½ a lemon
6 eggs, beaten

1. Heat the oil in a large, heavy skillet. Sauté the tomatoes, onion, and chiles until limp and "saucey."
2. Add the shredded beef and lime juice and continue to cook for several minutes more to meld the flavors.
3. Add a bit of oil to the pan if it looks too dry and stir in the beaten eggs. Cook, folding with a light hand, until the egg is soft and spongy. Serve at once with hot flour tortillas.

Close your eyes and think about sitting in the shadow of imposing Saddle Mountain (Cerro de la Silla) in downtown Monterrey. Now, think breakfast, open your eyes, and there on your plate is a steaming dish of red, gold, and green something with slivers of shredded beef. Pass the tortillas, you're about to eat Regiomontañes-style.

Note: You're allowed to substitute commercial dried beef. No, this dish has absolutely no taste relation to the infamous meal loathed by our Armed Forces—trust me!

---

[1] This dish is delicious without chilies too. Simply add a sprinkle of grated cheese and enjoy!

RAJAS ESTILO NORTEÑO

. . . .

Fried Chilies Poblano

Serves 6

12 Poblano chiles, roasted and peeled, or 1 large (26-ounce) can Jalapeños
½ cup olive oil
1 large white onion, sliced thin
½ cup each heavy whipping cream and sour cream (optional)
salt and pepper, to taste

1. Remove the seeds and veins from the chilies then cut them into 1½-inch strips. If using Poblanos you may want to soak them in vinegar water for half an hour to "tame" them. Dry the chilies well on paper towels.
2. In a heavy, medium-sized skillet, heat the oil and sauté the onion until transparent. Add the chilies and cover and cook over a low flame for about 10 minutes, stirring occasionally so they do not burn.
3. If using cream, add here and simmer an additional 7–8 minutes. Season to taste.

"Rajas" means strips, and this simple way of preparing fresh Poblano peppers appears on almost every combination plate South of the Border. They are a great way to pep up a taco too . . . just layer a few into a warm tortilla with good things like chicken or beef, or use them alone as a quick snack. Careful if you're not a chile lover, no two peppers have the same f.q., (fire quotient). Note the optional creams; if you wish to smooth out the flavor and use the recipe as a side vegetable, add the creams and then call the dish, "Rajas con Crema."

SALSA BORRACHA

The traditional companion to barbequed lamb, found always on the tables of the outdoor rustic restaurants that ring the Mexican Capital.

"Drunken" Sauce

Yield: about 1½ cups

6 pasilla chiles, seeded and deveined
2 tablespoons olive oil
1 medium-sized white onion, quartered
½ cup orange juice
¾ cup beer or ¼ cup tequila
1 medium-sized onion, chopped fine
¼ teaspoon salt, or more to taste

1. Rinse and dry the chilies. Heat the oil and sauté chilies, moving them constantly until they turn a shade or two lighter. Remove to the glass jar of the blender.
2. In same oil, sauté the quartered onion and add to the blender jar with orange juice, and beer or tequila. Blend until evenly grainy, not smooth.
3. Remove to a glass or pottery container, add the chopped onion, and salt to taste.

POLLO FRITO ESTILO COAHUILA

Fried Chicken, Coahuila-style

Serves 4

The State of Coahuila's claim to fame is that it was the birthplace of Francisco Madero, the father and fire of the Revolution of 1910. Because of Madero's equal fame as a fine trencherman, and also because chickens co-exist with Mexican households everywhere, this unusual recipe might have been served at his table.

6 tablespoons vegetable oil
1 pound potatoes, peeled, boiled, and sliced into ½-inch rounds
½ pound zucchini, sliced in ½-inch rounds
1 No. 2 can plum tomatoes (2½ cups)
1 tablespoon minced onions
3 tablespoons olive oil
1 tablespoon wine vinegar
corn meal flour (*harina de nixtamal* or *harina masa*)
salt and pepper, to taste
1 young chicken, cut into 4 pieces, skin removed
8 outer romaine leaves, washed
oregano, to taste
chili powder, to taste (optional)

1. Heat half of the vegetable oil in a large, heavy skillet. Fry the potatoes. Add the zucchini and sauté until just done. Remove from the skillet and set aside. Do not wash the skillet.
2. Coarsely chop the tomatoes and mix with the minced onion, olive oil, and vinegar in a medium-sized bowl. Set aside. (You have made a kind of salad mixture here.)
3. Wash the chicken well and pat dry. Place the corn flour in a plastic bag. Add the chicken and shake each piece until well coated, pressing the flour into the chicken through the bag. Add the remaining oil to the skillet and heat. Braise the chicken pieces until brown, turning once. Cover, and allow to cook about 20 minutes or until done.
4. For serving, place the chicken pieces on a heated platter; put the hot potatoes and sliced zucchini on top, then add the cold tomato sauce. Sprinkle the top with oregano and chili powder. Garnish the platter with romaine leaves and serve with hot tortillas.

SOPA DE LA CENA

Supper-in-a-Bowl, Northern-style

Serves 6

> It can get cold in the mountains of the Northwest, logger's country, and a colorful, clay bowl of this typical soup/stew delight is more than welcome. Omit the chilies if you're not up to their bite, but consider that they can be more warming than any extra pair of socks!

2 pounds meaty (country-style) pork ribs, cut into individual ribs
1 medium-sized onion, thinly sliced
1 teaspoon salt
1 bay leaf
2 cloves garlic, peeled
water
3 tomatoes, peeled, cored, and chopped
1 teaspoon oregano
3 cups fresh sweet corn kernels
2–3 cups cooked white rice
4 serrano chilies, stemmed and minced
lime wedges

1. In a heavy soup pot, place the meat, onion, salt, bay leaf, and garlic cloves. Cover amply with water and bring to a boil. Cover, reduce heat, and simmer for 2 hours.

2. Cool soup and skim off the top fat. Add the tomatoes, oregano, and corn and simmer for 30 to 45 minutes longer. Remove the bay leaf and garlic cloves. Taste and add salt if necessary.

3. Apportion soup, meat, vegetables, and rice into heated, deep bowls. Serve with small bowls of chopped chilies, lime wedges, and hot tortillas.

FRIJOLES BORRACHOS

. . . .

Drunken Beans

Yield: 8 servings

1 pound pinto beans,
   undercooked slightly
   (see page 242)
2 large, fresh Jalapeño chilies,
   deveined, seeded, and
   chopped fine
1 bottle *xxx* or other dark beer
6 slices fatty bacon, cooked and
   crumbled
1 large white onion, chopped
4 cloves garlic, whole
1 15-ounce can of whole plum tomatoes, drained and chopped
salt and black pepper, to taste

1. Drain the beans and place in a bean pot with the chilies and beer. Bring to a simmer.
2. In a heavy skillet, cook the bacon until crisp. Drain on paper towels. Reserve 3 tablespoons of the fat.
3. In the same skillet, reheat the bacon fat and sauté the onion and garlic until transparent. Add the tomatoes and crumbled bacon and allow to simmer for several minutes.
4. Add the tomato mixture to the beans, adjust the seasoning with salt and pepper, and bring to a boil. Lower the heat immediately and allow to simmer covered, for about 30 minutes. If beans look too dry, add more beer to maintain the proper consistency. If they are too soupy, allow them to cook, uncovered, for a few minutes.

> *There are as many versions of this dish as there are cooks in Monterrey—the only constant in the recipe is that you must use the locally-brewed Cuautémoc beer for authenticity*
>
> *I like using the dark xxx or the hearty Nochebuena (Christmas beer), but have fudged and used Guiness' or Beck's Dark on occasion.*

POLLO MENONITA

Mennonite Chicken

Serves 6

2 frying chickens, cut up
1/4 teaspoon dried marjoram
1 teaspoon paprika
2 tablespoons parsley, chopped
    fine
1/4 teaspoon pepper
3 tablespoons flour
salt and pepper
1 stick (4 ounces) butter or
    margarine, melted
3 tablespoons bacon drippings
    (I substitute peanut oil)
1 cup heavy cream (can substi-
    tute low-fat ricotta)

The Mennonite colony in Ciudad Cautemoc pride themselves on having the best dairy cows in the country. The recipe for this chicken dish was given to me by Hermana Lottie— I'm not sure who is whose namesake, but I'd be proud to claim this simple dish as my own.

(Because the cooking of the sect is hardly slenderizing or artery opening, I've put substitutions for the fats in the list of ingredients.)

1. Wash and dry the chickens. In a plastic bag, mix the marjoram, paprika, parsley, pepper, and flour.
2. Melt the butter with the bacon drippings in a metal baking casserole large enough to fit the chicken pieces. Heat the oven to 325°F.
3. Dip the chicken pieces in the fats and then place them in the plastic bag of spices and flour to coat well. Shake the excess off in the bag.
4. Place the chicken in the casserole and bake uncovered for 1 1/4 hours. Remove from the oven, pour the cream over the chicken, cover, and bring to a simmer on top of the stove for some 15 minutes to meld the flavors. Watch to see that it does not burn. If it looks too dry, add chicken broth or more cream.
5. Serve with white rice and a crunchy green vegetable.

CARNE DE RES EN CHILE COLORADO

. . . .

Beef in Red Chile

Serves 6

2 pounds lean stewing beef, cut
  into manageable pieces
1 12-ounce bottle Mexican beer
1 teaspoon salt
3 colorado chiles (Anaheim
  chilies can be substituted)
1 cup water
1/2 teaspoon powdered cumin
1/2 teaspoon oregano
3 peeled garlic cloves
salt
3 tablespoons oil

Hermosillo, the Capital of Sonora is a singularly un-Mexican looking city with a singularly, super-Mexican attitude. What's theirs is "the most and the best," starting with the gargantuan flour tortillas, often filled with shreds of beef prepared in this very savory and macho way—I suppose you might say this is the closest Mexican dish to our very American, Chile con Carne.

1. Put the beef in a heavy saucepan and pour over the beer. Sprinkle with salt and bring to a boil; then reduce the heat to a simmer. Cover and cook until tender (about 2 hours) and the liquid is nearly cooked away. When cool, shred and reserve. Do not wash the skillet.

2. Core, seed, and devein the chiles and place in a saucepan with water. Cover and simmer for 10 minutes, then transfer the chilies and water to the glass jar of a blender.

3. Add the cumin, oregano, and garlic. Blend until smooth, adding salt to taste.

4. In the heavy skillet in which the meat was cooked, heat the oil. Add the chile purée and sauté for 3 to 4 minutes. Add the meat and heat through, coating the meat with the purée. (Add a little more beer or water if needed.) Serve with warm, flour tortillas spread with refried beans (page 28).

MIGAS NORTEÑAS

Mexican Brunch Eggs

Serves 3–4

3 tablespoons vegetable oil
1 clove garlic, peeled and
    mashed
1 medium-sized onion,
    chopped fine
1 large tomato, peeled, chopped
    coarsely, and drained
1 sweet green pepper, chopped
1 sweet red pepper, chopped
2 canned Jalapeño peppers, or
    1 fresh (optional)
1 cup chopped ham
1 package nacho-type corn
    chips
6 eggs, well beaten
grated sharp Cheddar cheese
salt and pepper, to taste
    (optional)

Migas *translates to "crumbs." This is a favorite Northern Mexican breakfast . . . perhaps it was concocted by the hardy ranchers of Durango and Chihuahua. Imagine sitting in the Presidente Hotel dining room in Durango city, watching film crews and shoot-em-up stars breakfast on this savory specialty. Hollywood's cameramen swear by the pure light of the badlands-like environs. Exiting town towards the border you'll see one-dimensional film sets studding vast stands of cacti.*

1. In a large, heavy skillet, heat the oil. Lightly brown the garlic and onion. Add the tomato, green pepper, red pepper, and optional Jalapeño pepper. Allow to sauté while flavors meld. Add the chopped ham and stir mixture lightly until heated through.
2. If the corn chips are salted, empty them into a colander and shake vigorously to remove the excess salt. Set aside.
3. Beat the eggs well, pour over the vegetables, and fry quickly, folding until they are half cooked. Add the nachos, fold into the egg mixture, and finish cooking quickly. (Nachos should not be allowed to get soggy.)
4. Sprinkle liberally with grated cheese and serve at once.

Note: If you must hold these for a few minutes, place in an ovenwear casserole and put under the broiler, watching to see that they do not char. The final result should be browned and chewy.

CECINA

Half-Dried Beef

Yield: 1½ pounds (approximately)

2 pounds eye round of beef
2 tablespoons lemon or lime
    juice
2 teaspoons dried oregano
2 teaspoons kosher salt
vegetable oil

1. Have the butcher trim the thinner ends of the round and then trim crosswise with the grain to "butterfly" it. Have him repeat the process until he has the entire round laid out to ⅛-inch thickness. (If you tell him you're making "jerky," and he's an old timer, he'll know exactly what you want.)
2. Slice the beef into strips 6–8 inches long and 2 inches wide.
3. Mix the juice, oregano, and salt, and dip each strip into the mixture. Lay out on a cookie sheet, taking care that the strips do not touch each other. Refrigerate for several hours or over night.
4. Bake in a very low (200°F) oven until the meat is dry and hard. With a pastry brush coat lightly with oil and store in a tightly covered container.

Dried beef, or jerky as we call it, has long been a staple of the outdoorsman. In the outreaches of Mexico, where refrigeration is not always available, the drying of meat for long-term storage, is common. Cecina is dried for a shorter period of time and kept soft with oil.

Dozens of savory dishes are made with this staple of northern kitchens; the meat may be shredded and mixed with scrambled eggs (see "Machaca con Huevo," page 42) for a savory breakfast or light supper. It is also delicious mixed with chopped olives, raisins, and a tomatoey chili sauce and used as an irresistible taco filling.

Variation: In some parts of Mexico, Cecina is made with Adobo (see page 110) and stacked like a tall club sandwich, layer after layer, for storage and to intensify the flavor.

ARROZ HUÉRFANO

Rice with Bacon and Nuts

Serves 4–6

1 pound lean bacon
8 cups cooked white rice
  (see page 132)
½ cup pine nuts
½ cup pecans, shelled and
  broken

Huérfano, *means "orphan,"
and the connection with this
dish and its odd name probably derives from the fact that
a large bowl of this filling dish
could reasonably fill the yawn-
ing belly of the hungriest raga-
muffin. The recipe is my own
re-creation from the house
specialty at Saltillo's rustic
restaurant, La Canasta.*

1. Cook the bacon strips. Drain the fat and reserve. Pat the bacon dry between paper towels and crumble. Put the greasy towels to one side.
2. Prepare the white rice as in the basic recipe, substituting bacon fat for cooking oil.
3. With the bacon fat-greased paper towel, gently wipe the interior of a nonstick skillet and heat. Toast the pine nuts and pecans over medium heat, shaking the pan frequently to keep the nuts from burning.
4. Toss the rice with the bacon and nuts. Serve at once.

ELOTE ESTILO DURANGO

Corn-on-the-Cob, Durango-style

Serves 8

8 ears of tender corn
1 cup mayonnaise
1 cup coarse (kosher) salt
1 cup grated cheese
chili powder in a shaker
(optional)

1. Husk and remove the silk from the corn. Boil or steam until just tender.
2. Put the mayonnaise, salt, and grated cheese in separate oval dishes or bowls.
3. Place the shaker of chili powder close to where you plan to eat the corn.
4. Remove the corn from the water, quickly roll in mayonnaise, then salt, and finally in the grated cheese. Shake off the excess and season with chili powder if desired.

Enjoy . . . I told you it was messy!

The capital city of Durango has a handsome main square (zócalo). It is dominated by the 18th-century cathedral which looks out on a bandstand crowned by the legendary Mexican eagle and serpent.

Around the square are the usual small stands (puestos), selling this delicious snack. Vendors scoop the steaming ears from salvaged oil drums of boiling water and then twirl them in dishes of the condiments of choice: mayonnaise, chile, coarse salt, and grated cheese.

This is really not a recipe, more a plan of action. Also, it is definitely not a dish to eat elegantly—if you have a moustache or beard, you may want to hide behind a tree. Be prepared to have globs of the dry ingredients all over your face and hands, but what a treat!

CREPAS DE CAJETA DOÑA ROSARIO

. . . .

Caramel Crepes

Serves 8: 16 5-inch crepes

3/4 cup sifted all-purpose flour
1/2 teaspoon salt
1 teaspoon baking powder
2 eggs, well beaten
1 cup milk
2 tablespoons melted butter
4 teaspoons lemon zest
cooking oil
cajeta[1]
1 cup pecans, chopped

1. Sift the dry ingredients together into a medium-sized bowl.
2. Beat the eggs, milk, butter, and lemon zest. Pour into a well in the middle of the dry ingredients and beat until smooth.
3. Heat a crepe pan or 6-inch iron skillet (a drop of water sizzles and skitters across the pan). Add a few drops of oil. Pour about 3 tablespoons of the batter into the pan, quickly tilting to fill the entire bottom of the pan with the batter. Allow to cook until lightly browned. Turn the crepe over and brown the other side.
4. Reoil the pan for each crepe. Keep warm by covering with aluminum foil.
5. On heated dessert plates, spread each crepe with *cajeta*,[2] roll in powdered sugar, top with chopped pecans, and serve warm. Serve 2 per person.

For an unsettled year, my family and I lived in a suburb of the industrial city of Monterrey. Before the days of central air conditioning, we were miserable in the heat and dust, and fearful of the endless variety of insect and reptilian life that inhabited our garden.

My greatest glimmer of joy was in the weekly Wednesday, "salon," held by the Grande Dame of Monterrey society, Doña Rosario Garza Sada. Artists, musicians, and intellectuals visiting the fine "Tecnológico de Monterrey" were her guests, as well as this homesick-for-México City, gringa who lapped up her kindness. This recipe for a typical sweet she often served, is dedicated to my memories of a gracious lady.

Note: To store crepes, pile one on top of the other with sheets of waxed paper between each crepe. Crepes may be made in advance and frozen in this way. They keep for months in the freezer or a week in the refrigerator.

---

[1] Cajeta is a very sweet, creamy, caramel paste made from either cows' or goats' milk. It is a great favorite in all of Latin America, comparable to our passion for peanut butter. It is available in Hispanic groceries.
[2] You may substitute a favorite jam (I use Mango) or chopped fresh strawberries.

HOW SWEET IT IS!

The Latin-American penchant for sugar is well documented. Speaking with a soft-drink executive one day in Mexico City, he told me that the formulae for cola drinks in Hispanic countries, contained as much as 40 percent more sweetening than that of the United States.

There also seems to be a correlation between the avid consumption of hot or spicy food and the passion for a sweet, used as a fire extinguisher perhaps? Remember, that both sugar and chile are said to purvey endorphins, those invisible but comforting elements in our bodies which combat pain and give comfort!

The pre-hispanic dweller of Tenochtitlán had not yet learned the uses of cane sugar. The Conquistadores knew the pleasures of sweets from the Arabs and the Jews. The secrets of their preparation were not brought to this continent until the Spanish settlers brought with them nuns, wives, and daughters.

A largely unappreciated category of ethnic specialities is the variety of regional Mexican candies. It seems the early Mexican's natural sweet tooth couldn't wait until Cortes' arrival. He used honey and various sweet saps derived from cacti to create his singular confections.

One of these early delights was called *alegría* (happiness), and it is still enjoyed today in its original form. There is also a Mexican version of peanut brittle called *palanquetas*; and *ates* (a pressed fruit bar), exquisite; *cajeta* (a burned, caramel paste made from goat's milk), and dozens more in this category of *dulces* are savored today—made in the identical way they were almost 400 years ago.

An odd bit of food trivia however, is that although cocoa was an Aztec favorite consumed as a beverage, and the bean is grown all through Central and South America, chocolate is not the premier choice for desserts—indeed it is rarely used as a dessert ingredient.

FRIENDLY ENEMIES

"Señora . . . SeñoraaaaaH!!!! *El niño dice . . . que su* **Mamá**
le dijo!"

(Señora, . . . the child says that *you* said he **could***!*)

Every parent in Mexico has heard this plaint a dozen times a day
or more, depending upon the number of wily offspring involved. How
quickly the little "angelitos" learn to weasel and manipulate their hapless
"Nanas" and the rest of the household helpers. Kids are smart!

So you straighten it out, and you make it very clear, that you
NEVER said any such thing.

"Conchita, you are intelligent enough to know that I wouldn't
give permission for him to try climbing the glass-shard-edged roof bare-
foot to see how the Indian Fakirs do it."

"*Si Señora, pero él dijo . . .*" (. . . but he said . . .)

"Conchita, he's only *four*!!!!"

The relationship between the gentle Mexican house servants and
their charges is definitely adversarial; and they test and test and test . . .
BOTH groups of them. The kids try to see just how far they can go, and
"*las muchachas,*" follow along to see how far you'll *let* them go (that
refers both to their charges and themselves!).

The stories which have to do with child rearing in a Latin American country are legion, and I'd like to share a favorite with you.

Middle son Jeremy was a heller, all the more so because he
was an intelligent child. He could dream up the most inventive mischief.
One day after he had been the subject of at least a dozen of the above kind
of dialogs, he wandered sullenly off to the garden to lick his wounded
pride. The score had been: His Nana, 12 . . . Jeremy, zero.

The household buzzed along in the ensuing quiet. The tortillas
were delivered to the front door which always caused a stir because it
involved the dogs who bounded out for their tasty bribe, and a lengthy
"catch-up" on the latest neighborhood gossip via the cook's partyline. The
upstairs girl was outside, chatting with Roberto the gardener, while tend-
ing sheets in the brilliant, bleaching sun. The kitchen was temporarily
unattended.

Like most small boys, Jerry had a fascination with things wriggly. Sow bugs or potato bugs as some of you know them were particular favorites of his. He liked they way they rolled up into little balls when you poked them. We always made sure that the pockets of his jeans were emptied before washing lest we launder the insect population of his britches too.

Now where are we in this story? Here we have two dynamite elements; an imaginative small boy and an unmanned kitchen. Sauntering in, antennae alert for sweet revenge on his Nana, my son noted that a skillet was simmering. Pulling a stool up to the stove, he lifted the cover and inhaled the tempting fragrance of the afternoon's black *refritos*. Not hesitating, he dug for a handful of his little grey friends, popped them into the iron pan, stirred, returned the cover, and skedaddled for his room.

An hour later he had his grilled chop, mashed potatoes, and carrot sticks. He refused an offer of "refritos" which he normally consumed with zest, and then hung around the kitchen chatting with the cook. He stayed for the huge, midday servants' lunch pulling up that infamous stool, to "keep them company."

When they had scraped the final rice, beans, and leftover gravy from their plates, he made his move:

"Les gustaron los frijolitos hoy?" (You liked the beans today?) His seraphic, gap-toothed smile would have melted an ice sculpture.

Only when they had concurred that they had been unusually tasty, did he gleefully announce that they had eaten, with gusto, several dozens of his favorite entomological playmates.

"Señora . . . Señoraaaah . . ."

EL PACIFICO

States of:

SINALOA,
NAYARÍT,
JALISCO,
COLIMA

THE PACIFIC

Wouldn't geography study be a lot easier if countries, states, territories, cities, and towns were all laid out geometrically on grids? That would leave just islands with haphazard shapes and boundaries. Just a few, untidy floating-entities with which to deal.

One of the reasons why a strict delineation of the regions of Mexico is always a source of contention is the customary, sloppy irregularity of boundary lines. The *Pacífico* could include the enormous State of Sonora, which does indeed have a long Pacific coastline, but the food is Northern in influence. Moving down past Colima, all the way to the Guatemalan border, the azure Pacific does indeed lap for many kilometers. Let's just leave it at that—*my* Mexican Pacific is as advertised in the subheading!

This again is farming country and, in particular, produce. Vast stretches are given to the cultivation of asparagus, artichokes, rice, beans, peanuts, and grains, and of course, a dozen or more varieties of chili peppers, both hot and sweet. The very air smells of kitchen garden excess.

The ocean and the mouth of the Gulf of California teem with edible and sporting fish. Marlin and tuna will often be smoked for flavor and longer storage, while what we have come to call "trash fish" (pout, snook, and dogfish) are succulently prepared in a dozen different ways, depending on the ancestral recipes of the pueblo in which each individual cook operates.

Sinaloa's Mazatlán, translated from the Náhuatl, means "Place of the Deer." However, the only wildlife hunters to be seen these days are armed with rod and reel. Mazatlán is a fisherman's haven, both commercial and sport. Most of the frozen Mexican shrimp marketed in America come into the port for processing.

The town itself is the destination of endless bargain tours, and to my taste, its only attraction for historical purposes would be a stroll through noisy, malodorous Old Town for the fiery *caldo de camarón* (shrimp broth) in Carlos Anderson's "Shrimp Bucket in the Siesta Hotel. Mamucas and Doney restaurants are inexpensive and authentic.

Sábalo Beach, to the north of the city, has the pleasant Camino Real, Don El Guía, and newer El Pescador Hotels, perfect for an overnight to watch the sunset and the stunning black and white sea kites, who look like giant swallows in tuxedos as they catch the air currents and scout for their finny dinners.

Nayarít is a place of many mysteries; and the home of the reclusive Cora and Huichol Indians. Both cultures are master embroiderers, and a full Huichol costume, worn by the men of the tribe, may today cost thousands of dollars, if a collector is lucky enough to find one for sale.

These two dwindling cultures are extremely religious, celebrating a confusing blend of Catholic and pagan. Medicine men enter into lengthy trances to foretell the future, induced by the revered fungus, peyote. The holy men who practice these rituals enter into a period of abstinence and meditation for days before the actual rites.

For many, one of the most exciting traditions of Mexico is the Mariachi band. Jalisco is the home of this sentimental, demonstrative, musical art form.

In the hands of a master, dressed in tight black, studded with real silver, the Mariachi trumpet keens and caresses. Many a young Señorita has been seduced by an early-morning serenade (*gallo*), under her window.

Guadalajara is the mother lode of two extraordinary soups which are now enjoyed throughout the country; *Birria* and *Pozole*. Both of these meals-in-a-bowl require asbestos palates and strong digestive systems, but what a way to go!

It is also the grandstand of the *Charros*, the elitist society of horse owners and riders who wear a year's wages in silver on their incredible costumes and fifty pound sombreros. If you can be in the city during the October *charreada* (rodeo), you'll not only see these extraordinary riders and ropers perform and compete, but you'll be able to appreciate some of the finest horseflesh in the world. Horse buying and trading goes on during these special days, and everyone and everything is "on stage"—exciting!

The tiny state of Colima is agricultural and generally unpretentious. It is also plagued by hurricanes and voracious black flies. The only bow to glitz is the Las Hadas resort, a pseudo Shangri-la just outside the city of Manzanillo. It typifies the "It's a fun place to visit, but I wouldn't want to stay there."

THINGS TO SEE, DO, AND EAT

Tepic: The Regional Museum contains some unusual Classical Period pieces (400–600 A.D.), depicting life in the pre-Columbian "raw." Sculptures of medical anomalies and exuberant love-making are among the treasures in this poorly-organized but worth-the-visit, government holding.

San Blas: A scenically glorious beach, but this is the beginning of the land of the *Jején* or "no-see-ums" as Americans call them. Always travel in Mexico with your own spray insecticide (ceilings are high in most hotel rooms) and lotion. The entire Nayarít coast is paralleled by mangrove swamps, and the combination of the brackish water and the sea make for an insect's Eden.

If Sinaloa and Nayarít have little to recommend them for civilized travellers, then Jalisco's bounty takes up the slack. We'll stay on the coast for a bit:

Puerto Vallarta: Of course the beach, and of course, try the stick-skewered fish cooked over charcoal. The snorkeling and scuba diving is sensational (check with the concessionaire on **Playa de los Muertos**; all equipment can be rented). There are dozens of fine restaurants, my favorite for lunch being **Chico's Paradise**, which is a taxi ride out of town.

Shopping, oh my! There is a clutch of irresistible shops on Calle Corona; everything from **Josefa's** wonderful, hand-embroidered and appliquéd designs (men and women's), to Mexican contemporary art; a gallery of Huichol art and another dedicated to masks from around the world. Bring money!

Inland towards Guadalajara enjoy a five-hour drive inland from the azure Pacific. As the second largest city in the Republic, the city suffers from all of the evils of "too fast, too much," particularly when speaking of population figures and the ensuing pollution problem common to all of the cities in Mexico. On the other side of the scale is the great charm of the **Tapatíos**, their obvious pride in their surroundings and traditions and the beauty of her Colonial heart. In her environs you'll find:

Hospicio de Cabañas: The powerful murals of **José Clemente Orozco** are here and can be studied prone, with wooden benches supplied to keep you from "Sistine Chapel" neck cramps. Purchase a pamphlet (they have them in several languages) explaining the frescoes, otherwise, they are overwhelming.

Museo Regional: They have good collection of pre-Columbian pieces, mixed with five rooms devoted to Spanish-influenced Colonial art.

Tlaquepaque: El Parián is the central plaza of this craft, and general shopping-haven. Plan a full morning (or more) to wander its maze, and stay to have lunch outdoors. Mariachi's, street vendors, and international tourists are the scene here.

Tonalá: This ancient pottery center holds market days on Thursdays and Sundays. Look for the old-fashioned, matte-finish figures of animals and birds, either free-standing, or depicted on the sides of graceful vases and water pitchers. When you get them home, spray them with transparent polyurethane and they will keep their subtle coloring for years.

Tequila: (Pronounced take-eel-a. Please don't make it rhyme with mantilla—it only has one "l.") The home of Mexico's fabled drink. Pass on the town, and buy your booze at the airport. It's not worth the unattractive trip, unless you're in the liquor business and want to see the industrialized process firsthand.

BACK TO THE SEA

Costa Careyes: A former pirates' hideaway, it is now the research center of marine biologists studying sea turtles *(caguama)* which use the beach as a nesting place. An elegant resort hideaway, Costa Careyes ignores science and the rest of the world.

Barra Navidad: Enjoy red snapper tacos at **Mariscos Nacho**. Cold marinated octupus is good too, washed down with a cold Pacífico *cerveza*. By the way, this is *guayaba* (a quince cousin) country—try any of the delicious ways it is offered.

Colima: Look for the masks of the Candelario family from Suchitlán in the **FONART** shop and elsewhere. If, in your secret heart, you're fascinated by vulcanology, the two local peaks, **Nevado de Colima** and **Volcán de Fuego**, are still simmering—unfortunately access is blocked by a private holding, but a telephoto lens can capture some spectacular views.

Manzanillo: Stop and have a frosty margarita at **Las Hadas resort**, just to say you've been there. For all its advertised glamour, it's usually hellishly hot, overrun with "wannabe celebrity" types, and outlandishly overpriced!

SOPA AGUADA

Everyday Noodle Soup

Serves 4

3 tablespoons vegetable oil
2 cloves garlic, peeled and
  mashed
½ pound vermicelli noodles
4 teaspoons powdered chicken
  soup base
6 cups water
salt and pepper, to taste

Desirable but optional:
2 carrots, peeled and chopped
1 large tomato, peeled and
  chopped
½ onion, chopped
meat bones or peeled chicken feet
parsley

This Sopa Aguada *(wet soup)* is cooked daily in the Mexican kitchen, and much can be told about the economics of the cook by its paucity or wealth of ingredients. One of the first things a country cook learns when she is employed in a city household, is to add a few vegetables and perhaps even meat or chicken bones to the mix . . . as typically in the poor provinces, this is really flavored water with a handful of vermicelli noodles.

1. In a 1½ to 2-quart saucepan, heat the oil and sauté the garlic and uncooked noodles until they are a light brown color.
2. Dissolve the chicken soup base in 1 cup of water. Add with the rest of the water to the noodles.
3. Bring to a boil and cook until the noodles are *al dente.* Taste and add salt and pepper, if desired.
4. For the richer soup prepare 2 more cups of broth and add any or all of the optionals to the 6 cups of broth. Cook for 20 minutes before adding to the noodle mix.
5. Remove bones or chicken feet and serve hot with warm rolls.

BIRRIA
TAPATÍA

No cookery book which includes the sophisticated cuisine of Guadalajara would be complete without mention of this soup/stew. The busy streets of Tlaquepaque, the city's center for crafts, are daily perfumed with *Birria*. Most popularly it is made with lamb, but in parts of the North, young kid is used for its pungent flavor.

The soup's history is an ancient one—it is said to date from pre-Hispanic times when it was originally made with the meat of the *Xoloescuintle*, the small hairless dogs which were raised like chickens for the Aztec tables.

The modern ingredients for this satisfying dish include: a five-pound chunk of mutton or goat, tomatoes, at least two kinds of chilies (of preference, anchos, and guajillos), onions, a hefty amount of fresh garlic, lemon juice or vinegar, and six or seven fragrant herbs (dried and fresh).

An *adobo* (see page 110) paste is made to slather the meat, which is then roasted in cactus leaves. In the meantime, all of the savory ingredients are flavoring the broth in which the meat will finally be served. This wonderful witches' brew simmers for several hours before receiving the shredded meat and the toppings of chopped onions, coriander/cilantro, and slices of limes.

The fragrance wafting from the restaurants specializing in this culinary work of art (*birrerías*), have waiting lines of customers at all hours of the day and night. Could it be because it is said to be a sure cure for a *cruda* (hangover)?

CAZUELA DE ELOTE COLIMENSE

Fresh Corn Tamale Casserole

Serves 6–8

12 ears corn
3 tablespoons vegetable oil
1 teaspoon baking powder
3 egg yolks, beaten
salt, to taste
1 boiled chicken or 3 boiled
chicken breasts, deboned and
shredded
3 cups *mole* sauce (see page 96
or use canned sauce

1. Cut the corn from cob and coarse grind 3/4 of the kernels in a food processor or blender. Drain excess liquid.
2. In a heavy skillet, heat the oil and quick sauté the ground corn and kernels, stirring consistently until translucent.
3. Remove from the heat, blend with the flour, baking powder, and egg yolks and beat for a few minutes with wooden spoon.
4. Put half of this mixture into a greased, ovenproof dish or casserole. Top with shredded chicken and then the *mole*. Top with the other half of the corn mixture and corn and bake in 350°F oven until cooked. (Test the top half of the dough with a cake tester, it should come out clean.)

Colima, named after a tribal king[1] of 13th-century Mexico, is an agricultural paradise, the site of an annual agricultural fair in November. The state scenically is very beautiful and delightfully ignored by the usual tourist guides. Take time to browse through the city's tiny Mask Museum,[2] the Museum of Western Culture, and the Casa de Cultura, then go have lunch at Los Naranjos. It's where the locals go, and it's consistently good.

Because Colima is corn country, this recipe represents a dish you might find in any of the local restaurants.

---

[1] King Colimotl, leader of the Tecos, a small peaceful tribe of the area, led an underdog victory in a battle against the Purépechas from the next-door State of Michoacán.
[2] The Mask Museum displays the work of the family of artisan Herminio Candelario, from nearby Suchitlán. The town itself is about a half hour's drive from the city of Colima, and for craft collectors, a must!

ROBALO EN SALSA DE PEREJIL

Sea Bass in Parsley Sauce

Serves 6

The Mexican seabass from the Gulf of California is a snowy-fleshed, but full-flavored fish. This rendering turns the calendar back to a gorgeous sunset enjoyed overlooking gorgeous Bacochi-bampo bay in Guaymas. The margaritas were icy and the fish succulent.

1 11-ounce can *tomatillos*
2 cloves garlic, minced
1 medium-sized onion, minced
1 cup parsley, finely chopped
2 tablespoons fresh coriander/cilantro leaves, chopped
¼ teaspoon ground cumin
2 tablespoons vegetable oil
salt and pepper, to taste
pat of butter or margarine
6 6-ounce fish fillets
juice 1 lemon
lemon wedges for garnish

1. Purée the tomatillos in a blender with their juice.
2. Combine the garlic, onion, parsley, coriander/cilantro, and cumin. Sauté lightly in oil. Combine with the tomatillo purée. Season to taste.
3. Butter a rectangular baking dish. Spread half of the parsley sauce over the bottom. Lay the fish fillets over the sauce. Cover the fillets with the remaining sauce.
4. Bake at 350°F for about 15 minutes or until fish flakes easily with a fork.
5. Serve at once, sprinkled with lemon juice and with lemon wedges on the side.

QUESO FUNDIDO TAPATÍO

Melted Cheese, Jalisco-style

Yield: 6–8 saucer-size servings

½ pound chorizo (a hot
  Italian sausage may be
  substituted)
4 large *tomatillos*, minced
1 medium-sized onion, grated
  or minced
1 pound Chihuahua or white Cheddar cheese, grated
1 small Oaxaca or mozzarella cheese, shredded
tortillas

Melted cheese in small clay pots or dishes is a common appetizer or "side" in many Mexican restaurants, but nowhere is it more delicious than in "Los Cazadores," in Guadalajara. The combination of bits of brilliant green tomatillos and tangy chorizo still titillate my cook's memory.

1. Peel the casing from the chorizo, break into pieces, and cook in a hot skillet until the meat is browned and all the fat is rendered. Drain the chorizo on paper towels and reserve 2 tablespoons of the fat to grease the individual serving dishes.

2. Sauté the tomatillos with the onion for several minutes in some of the chorizo fat. Drain.

3. Drizzle a small amount of fat into each serving dish and divide the cooked chorizo, tomatillo, and onion evenly into the dishes. Top with equal amounts of the 2 cheeses.

4. Bake in 375°F oven until the cheese is melted and bubbly. Serve with hot tortillas as an appetizer or as a topping for steak, Guadalajara-style.

PESCADO BLANCO LAGUNA

Freshwater Fish, Nayarít-style

Serves 4

12 white fish fillets
½ cup flour
½ cup light olive oil or sesame
  seed oil
4 cloves garlic, peeled and
  minced
1 tablespoon freshly grated
  ginger
juice of 6 limes
½ cup bread crumbs, toasted

The fish were small and white—and when I asked their name, I was told they were called, "white fish." (Aren't we tourists dumb sometimes!) The setting was a corner of paradise, the volcanic lagoon of Santa María del Oro near Ixtlán in Nayarít. Served on a cracked, white plate, nothing, not even their silvery, slumbering eyes could detract from their flavor.

You may want to try this simple preparation with some of the excellent farmed catfish now available everywhere.

1. Rinse the fillets, dry lightly, and coat both sides well with flour. Place on wax paper in the refrigerator while you prepare the following.
2. In a heavy skillet large enough to fry all of the fillets, heat the oil and lightly brown the garlic and the ginger (stay with it, it burns in a wink).
3. Lay the fish fillets in the garlic/ginger oil and brown on both sides, turning once. Remove to a heated platter and sprinkle with the lime juice and toasted bread crumbs.

ENSALADA DE PAPAS CON CHIPOTLE

. . . .

Spicy Potato Salad

Serves 6

8 red Bliss potatoes
6 tablespoons wine vinegar
1 large sweet onion, grated
6 tablespoons olive oil
salt and pepper, to taste
4 canned chipotle peppers,
    seeded, deveined and julienne
12 large romaine leaves
4–6 ounces of Feta or similar fresh cheese
handful of watercress as a garnish

This salad is for the true lover of "Le Food Hot!". The combination of bland potatoes, salty cheese, and the bite of the chipotles is not to everyone's taste, but it is a family favorite of ours. This recipe is an "evolved" one, originally served to us in a tiny, birrería in Tonalá, Jalisco just down the street from the Thursday pottery market.

1. Boil the potatoes in their skins. When cool enough to handle, cut into bite-sized pieces and toss with 4 tablespoons vinegar.
2. Whisk together the onion, olive oil, remaining vinegar, and salt and pepper. Add a few drops of the chipotle oil if you want a bit more bite, and pour over the potatoes.
3. Fold in the chipotles and adjust the seasoning. Allow to sit at room temperature for an hour.
4. Arrange a bed of romaine leaves. Spoon the salad on top and sprinkle liberally with the cheese. Garnish with watercress sprigs and serve.

FRITURAS DE COLIFLOR

Cauliflower Fritters

Serves 6

1 cauliflower, divided into
    flowerets
1 tablespoon vinegar (any kind)
½ pound Feta-type cheese
1 cup flour for dredging
3 eggs, well beaten
¼ cup vegetable oil
½ medium-sized onion, minced
1 clove garlic, mashed
3 cups tomato sauce (any kind)
1 teaspoon minced parsley
½ teaspoon chili powder
¼ teaspoon cumin
salt, to taste

Mexican cooks do magical things with very ordinary vegetables. Here the snowy cauliflower that is grown in the northern Pacific coast area, is converted into a colorful and super-savory side or main dish. The same modus operandi, works well with zucchini— simply make little sandwiches of zucchini rounds with cheese in the middle and tack together with a toothpick. Remove the toothpick before serving.

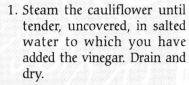

1. Steam the cauliflower until tender, uncovered, in salted water to which you have added the vinegar. Drain and dry.

2. Divide the cauliflower into medium-sized pieces. Open little spaces in the flowerets with a fork and tuck in small slivers of cheese. Dredge each floweret in flour, shake off excess, and then dip in beaten eggs.[1]

3. In a heavy skillet, heat the oil until a drop of water added sizzles and pops. Gently add the fritters to the oil and fry until golden brown. Set aside on paper towels.

4. Pour out all but a tablespoon of oil. Sauté the onion and garlic. When soft, add the tomato sauce, parsley, and seasonings. Simmer for 10 minutes.

5. Place the fritters on a heated serving dish and pour over the hot tomato sauce. Garnish with more crumbled cheese.

---

[1] This sounds backwards to many of us, but it is the way the Mexican cook breads things. The results are a puffy, outside coating that is delicious.

CORNY
AS HELL!

7,000-Year-Old Grain

The tourist to Mexico knows the regional name of "Tehuacán," as the bottled bubbly which one is advised to drink to keep the stomach demons at bay. To food historians Tehuacán is the valley where corn was first cultivated ... the time frame? ... 6,000–5,000 B.C.

Consider that corn is the only grain that cannot reproduce itself, but must be harvested and planted every season—it is the lifework of millions of indigenous farmers, dedicated to the task of keeping the vital and succulent grain growing. More food for thought—no one in the world scientific communities knows from where the first corn plant sprang; it does not grow wild and the origins of the mutant(?), hybrid(?) are still an agricultural and botanical mystery.

No mystery at all, is the ancient dependency of Meso-America on the flavorful grain and its by-products. Religious observances which spoke to the corn Gods, Centeocíhuatl, Xilonen, Llametecuhtli, Chicomecóatl and many more, abounded in pre-Columbian times, and today continue in modified rites from Mexicali to the Yucatán peninsula. Corn is the great earth Mother whose capacity to nurture is unlimited.

BLUE CORN

Blue is a color associated with flowers, sky, and sea; but few edibles reflect this natural hue. Here again we have an example of Mexico's gift for artisanry of all kinds, including things edible . . . blue corn is definitely "in!"

A cousin to the native North American, Indian corn, blue corn is a mutant strain much prized by the Hopi, Navajo, and Pueblo peoples. Author Carolyn Niethammer in her book *American Indian Food and Lore* (Collier Books) notes that " . . . the flavor is superior to that of white or yellow corn. Ashes of various plants . . . are used so the corn will remain blue and not turn green or gray."

Blue tortillas made from the dark grey-blue ears are found all over Mexico but most commonly in the states of Morelos, Guerrero, and Puebla. Generally, the more common, beige freckled tortillas come steaming to the table three or four times a day. In more citified areas, the occasional multi-colored ears may be tossed to the family porker.

As the making by hand of tortillas falls before the clanking cacophany of the unbeautiful tortilla "machine" found in every pueblito, the incidence of blue tortillas or tamales (or any product that requires laborious hours bent over a volcanic stone *metate*), gracing the Mexican tables decreases drastically.

The use of ash substituting for the lime (*cal*), is common to Guanajuato and Michoacán, and the resulting greyish tortilla has a more delicate, smoky flavor. As a cottage craft, neither the grey nor the blue tortillas are available commercially in Mexico.

Things made with corn taste good . . . one of the reasons we are so impassioned about Mexican cuisine! Here is a sampling of the over 500 uses to which Mexican cooks over the centuries have put their favored grain:

Atole: Flavored, corn-based beverage or gruel.

Frituras: Fritters.

Tamales: Cornmeal dumplings, variously spiced or sweet; steamed in corn husks or other leaves.

Tortillas: The Mexican staff of life. Thin, ground corn (mixed with lime or ash) pancakes or crepes. Eaten plain or filled, with the hands.

Taco: Tortilla wrapped filling (beans, cheese, meat, vegetables), eaten with the hands.

Enchilada: Taco, covered with sauce. Eaten, with utensils.

Garnachas: Small (3- to 4-inch diameter), thick corn-dough pancakes with a turned-up "lip" to hold various sauces or fillings. Served as an appetizer.

Gorditas: ("Little Fat Ones") small, chunky corn cakes, baked on a griddle *(comal)*. Often flavored with molasses-sugar *(piloncillo)*.

Quesadillas: This translates to "little cheese things," but the tortilla "turnovers" may be filled with ham, potatoes, vegetables, and of course, various cheeses.

Tostada: A crisp toasted tortilla used as a base for shredded lettuce, refried beans, avocado, meat, chicken, or whatever the imagination and the mouth opening allows.

CHILES RELLENOS LOS MOCHIS

Bean Stuffed Chilies

Serves 6

Los Mochis is an ugly little mining town, and a terminus for several transportation lines. Avoid it if you can. For many years it was the home of a talented sculptor friend of mine, Naomi Siegmann, and this recipe from the area is dedicated to her talent and forbearance.

1 pound light-colored beans
(such as pintos or navy)
1 pound of chorizo
1 small can chipotle chilies,
seeded and rinsed
1 pound Chihuahua or white Cheddar cheese, grated
12 fresh Poblano chilies[1] (choose straight ones, not the curled)
2 cups sour cream

1. Cook the beans (see page 133). Purée in a processor or blender.
2. Strip the outside skin from the chorizo, mash, and fry until dry and crispy. Drain away the fat and add the chorizo to the beans.
3 Chop the chipotle chilies into large dice. Blend together with the bean mixture and the cheese.
4. In a hot, nonstick fry pan, toast the whole Poblano chilies on both sides, pressing them flat with a spatula. Remove from the heat, slit each chile, and remove the seeds. Carefully stuff the prepared Poblano chilies with the bean-cheese mixture.
5. Grease an ovenware casserole. Place the chilies, stuffing side up, in the casserole. Cover with the sour cream.
6. Bake at 375°F until heated through and bubbly about 30–40 minutes. Serve at once.

---

[1] Sweet green or red peppers may be substituted for a milder dish.

ENCHILADAS ESTILO TONALÁ

Enchiladas, Tonalá-style

Serves 6 as an appetizer

2 sweet peppers
2 medium-sized tomatoes, peeled
1 medium-sized onion
1/2 cup vegetable oil
2 tablespoons milk
1/4 cup sour cream or crème fraîche
1 teaspoon tequila
salt
6 tortillas
lettuce leaves
whole radishes for garnish

Filling:
juice of 1 lemon
1 large avocado, chunked
2 sweet peppers, chopped
1/2 cup fresh cheese (Feta does nicely), crumbled
8 radishes, chopped coarsely

Tonalá has long been a destination for lovers of unusual pottery. Before things got too commercial, the craftsmen made stunning vases, decorative water filters, and figurines. Flowers and mythical animals disported themselves across unglazed surfaces painted in soft earth hues of brown, ochres, and grey-blue. Today you really have to search for practitioners of the old art.

Thursday and Sunday are market days. On other days you may be misled to think the town deserted, but I assure you, brisk bargaining is going on behind the battered zaguanes (huge wooden entrance doors) of the town. Give a youngster five pesos, walk your fingers in the air, (the Mexican hand signal for "take me to" and say to him—"Artesanos de barro, los buenos." If you look adventuresome to him, he may lead you to an artisan who deftly fashions pornographic images in clay. Look stern, say, "No, no, esa no!," and in a firm voice repeat "Cerámica fina."

1. Remove the seeds from the sweet peppers and chop the tomatoes and onion.
2. In a large skillet, heat the oil and sauté the peppers, tomatoes, and onion until limp. Simmer this sauce about 2 minutes. Add the milk, sour cream, tequila, and salt to taste.
3. To make the filling, toss the lemon juice with the avocado. With a fork, blend the avocado, peppers, cheese, and radishes. Set aside.
4. Dip each tortilla in sauce, place a tablespoon of the filling on each, and roll.
5. Serve immediately on top of a lettuce bed adorned with whole radishes.

Note: Because enchiladas *have sauce, they are eaten with a fork.* Tacos, *on the other hand are finger food.*

POZOLE TAPATÍO

Pork and Hominy Stew

Serves 4–6

In Guadalajara, the birthplace of this soup which is enjoyed everywhere, the stock is started with a hog's head. Realizing the difficulty of securing one in most places, plus the natural squeamishness of many cooks about cooking things that stare back, I've always substituted pig's feet. I also admit to cheating with the hominy— I save time by using the canned product.

6 quarts water
3 pounds country-style pork
   ribs
2 pigs feet, cleaned and halved
6 chicken legs and thighs
4 cloves garlic, mashed
1 medium-sized onion
3 ancho chilies, seeded and
   deveined
1 teaspoon Tabasco or other hot
   sauce
2 16-ounce cans of white hominy, drained
2 tablespoons wine vinegar
salt and pepper, to taste

Garnishes:
½ head cabbage, finely shredded
12 radishes, sliced thin
1 cup scallions, chopped
handful of coriander/cilantro, chopped course
wedges of lime
small bowl of dried oregano
crisp fried tostadas (tortilla quarters)

1. In a large soup pot, put the water, hominy, pork ribs, pigs feet, chicken legs and thighs, garlic, and onion. Bring to a rolling boil, skim off the fat and reduce the heat. Cover and cook over medium heat for 1½–2 hours.

2. Break the chilies into pieces and toast both sides until they blister on a griddle or in a heavy skillet. In a small bowl, cover with hot water until they soften.

3. Drain all but ½ cup of water from the chilies and purée with vinegar in a glass jar of a blender. Put in a strainer and with a spoon, push through into the simmering broth. Add Tabasco or other hot sauce, and stir. Taste for seasoning. Simmer for 45 minutes.
4. Add canned hominy and continue cooking for 15 minutes.
5. Remove pork, chicken, and bones. When cool enough to handle, shred the meats and discard the cartilage and bones. Check the soup seasoning again (hominy soaks up salt like a sponge) and correct if necessary. Place the meat in a large sieve over the hot soup, submerge several times to get it hot, and then let it drain over the pot.
6. Divide the meat among the large, heated soup bowls. Pour the soup on top and garnish with the cabbage and radishes. Serve with the rest of the garnishes passed separately.

PEZ VELA CON JITOMATE

Sailfish with Tomato Sauce

Serves 6

6 cups water
6 cloves garlic, 3 whole,
   3 chopped
1 small onion
1 small sprig thyme
   (¼ teaspoon dried)
1 small sprig marjoram
   (¼ teaspoon dried)
1½ teaspoons salt
2 pounds fish fillet (sailfish,
   swordfish, or marlin), cut
   into 6 pieces
4 tablespoons vegetable oil
1 cup onion, minced
6 tomatoes, peeled and chopped
3 black peppercorns
1 whole clove
½ teaspoon ground cumin
¼ cup red wine vinegar
½ cup parsley, chopped fine
1 tablespoon dried oregano
3 tablespoons chopped *epazote*,
   optional (see page 20)
4 pickled chiles Jalapeños,
   chopped
2 tablespoons pickled chile juice
low fat sour cream

My first taste of this dish was inland from the sea, in Tepic (perhaps the fish "sailed" over the terrible road from Santa Cruz). We sat at a small table in the Sierra de Alica Hotel and planned our next adventure. Because native crafts are our passion, we had checked with the tourist office next door as to which day was a market day or a festival day in Jésus María, where native embroideries and wool "paintings" are sold.

With permission from the INI[1] you may be able to "puddle jump" into Cora and Huichol Indian country. If you can wangle permission, follow the rules, be respectful, and no cameras. Also, double check the flight schedules, they can be erratic.

---

[1] Instituto Nacional Indigenista, the Mexican equivalent of the U.S. Office of Indian Affairs.

1. Place the water, whole garlic cloves, onion quartered, thyme, marjoram, and 1 teaspoon of the salt in a large pot or Dutch oven. Bring the water to a boil, add the fish, cover, lower heat and poach over medium heat for 6–8 minutes or until the fish can be easily pierced with a fork. Strain and reserve the fish stock.
2. Heat the oil in a large saucepan, add the chopped onion and garlic and sauté until transparent. Add the tomatoes, peppercorns, clove, cumin, vinegar, and the remaining 1/2 teaspoon salt and sauté for 5 minutes, stirring constantly.
3. Add the fish, parsley, oregano, *epazote*, chiles, and chile juice. Allow to cook for 3 minutes adding from the fish stock if necessary. Cover and simmer for 5 minutes. Mixture should be almost mushy. Serve hot over Mexican rice garnished with a dollop of sour cream.

Makes an excellent taco filling also.

GUAYABAS BAHÍA NAVIDAD

Stuffed Guavas, Christmas Bay-style

Guavas grow on small, shrub-like trees, and looking down on the Navidad lagoon with your back to the sea, you can see the shiny-leaved foliage for miles as the plantings follow the curves of the hills.

Serves 6

12 large, ripe guavas
1½ cups brown sugar
1½ cups apple juice
4 Granny Smith apples, cored, peeled, and quartered
½ cup pecans, chopped fine
½ cup pecans, halved for garnish

1. Peel the guavas and place in ice water for 1 hour. Drain, cut in half lengthwise, and scoop out the pulp and seeds. Reserve.
2. In a covered saucepan, cook the guava halves over low heat until just tender, about 5 minutes. Remove and place in ice water.
3. Bring the sugar and apple juice to a boil, and add the guava pulp, simmering until reduced by half.
4. Place the apples in a medium-sized saucepan, cover with water, bring to boil, and drain. Add the apples to guava mixture and cook slowly until a paste consistency. Blend in the nuts.
5. Stuff the guava halves with the paste, fitting two halves together so that fruit appears whole. Chill and serve 1 whole guava per person on a plate sprinkled with additional nut halves.

TEPACHE

Pineapple Beer

Makes 5 + quarts

> *Now don't turn up your noses
> . . . a cold glass of Tepache on
> a sweltering day is a golden
> delight you may dream about
> for vacations to come. Try it
> for your next outdoor picnic or
> barbeque, remembering always
> that as long as it sits in the glass
> container, it will continue to
> ferment and get stronger!*

2 pounds brown sugar
4 quarts water
cinnamon, cloves, and anise,
   to taste
pinch of black pepper
1 medium-sized pineapple,
   peeled and ground
1 banana, mashed
1 quart of beer or 1 yeast cake

1. In a large saucepan, boil together for 5 minutes the brown sugar and water. Add the spices and boil for an additional 15 minutes. Cool.
2. Add the pineapple and banana and pour the mixture into a large earthen or glass crock (do not use metal). Add the beer or yeast and allow to ferment for 24 hours. Strain and chill.

GIVE US
THIS DAY

EL PAN—THE DAILY BREAD

In Mexico's history the Spaniards were most often the villains—the takers rather than the givers. The great exception to this rule was the introduction of bread into the culture of the Aztecs. Not only were the Iberians great bread eaters, but their priests taught the gospel of bread as the body of Christ.

Bread and its baking have certainly attained an apogean place in any history of Mexican food. One has only to wander the aisles of any urban bakery in the Hispanic land, tray in hand and serving pincers poised, to feel almost "through the looking glass." What a marvel of inventive craft—what mastery of an art form—what LOVE of product!

The names of the various breads in daily use are another enchantment: horns (animal, not musi-cal), flutes, spinning tops, shells, screws, cannons, Viennas, Pancho's eyes, braids, big bellies, country girls, and even "Semites" (*Semitas*). In total there are more than 500 different kinds of *pan diario*.

Holidays bring out the very best in the country's bakers. The colored sugar icings, a multitude of fanciful shapes and designs, and the variety of special content, fruits, nuts, party favors (watch how you bite!) boggles the mind and senses.

The commonest forms of bread are individual rather than loaf . . . they weigh about 30 grams (just over an ounce each). The obvious reason for this is the economy. No matter how poor, one can buy, or beg for, at least one *panecito*—the loss of dignity weighs as little as the precious mouthful—somehow a "loaf" of bread is another matter entirely—an ugly admission of poverty—remember, notwithstanding the bank balance, the Mexican is always very proud.

EL CENTRO

States of:

GUERRERO,
MÉXICO,
PUEBLA,
TLAXCALA,
HIDALGO,

MEXICO'S CUMMERBUND OF CULINARY DELIGHTS

The wide sash across the belly of the most populous section of Mexico, stretching from the Guerrero seacoast through the rice fields of Morelos and up into the high plateau of the State of Mexico, the Federal District, and Puebla is vibrantly colored with ethnic threads.

The well-known cities of Acapulco, Puebla, Cuernavaca, and the Capital (D.F.) itself, boast a special allure of multicultural mystery. This, of course, includes a variety of lodgings and foods to boggle the mind!

To the casual visitor, it would seem that the resort cities of Acapulco, Zihuatenejo, and Ixtapa, play all day and night, The dark faces of the Costa Brava, reflect the African influence, introduced during the rough and ribald, spice and slave trading days.

Behind the scenes, this mixture of traders' descendants are the owners and operators of the commercial centers—stores, markets, and small, support businesses which cater to the seasonal trade.

Lightening the mix is the omnipresent face of the resort visitor himself, enraptured by the bustle of these seaport centers; captivated by sunlight and exotic sights; eager to experience all that this part of the warm, azure Pacific offers.

On the other side of the behavioral spectrum is the City of Puebla, a strange combination of conservative Catholicism and indigenous excess. Everything from churrigueresque decor of the churches and cathedral to the enchanting use of the Talavera tile of the area, conspires to make one wonder and smile. So too does the elaborate cuisine of the state—from the famed *Mole Poblano* to the dozens of unusual sweets for which the city is reknowned.

Balmy Cuernavaca is a paean to the middle class of Mexico, their weekend retreat turned industrial center. Flower-laden in spite of the air pollution, its high-walled properties enclose small segments of paradise.

Included in this belt of geographic and ethnographic counterpoint are the small states of Tlaxcala and Hidalgo. Tlaxcala's claim to fame is the annual festival in which the avenue to the Monastery of San Francisco is carpeted with fresh flowers laid in intricate designs depicting church and town history. There is also a fine "living" crafts museum, where local artisans work and teach both students and public.

Hidalgo is mining country. Near Pachuca, two beautiful haciendas, San Miguel Regla and Santa María Regla, have been converted into splendid hostels, where the dramatic surroundings of the once silver-rich hills are worth an overnight. The cuisine in both hotels is unfortunately forgettable.

The State of Mexico (not to be confused with the capital city), which wraps itself completely around the Federal District (D.F.), is a notable food center. The enjoyment of her delicacies however—spicy sausage (*chorizo*), tacos with chili and tiny bits of potato, freshwater mini-shellfish *(acosiles)*, flavored fresh cheeses (*queso asadero*), which translates to "melting cheese"—is generally a "stand-up in the market" experience, not for ye of delicate digestion. The Friday market in Toluca attracts farmers, artisans, and visitors from miles around.

THINGS TO SEE, DO, AND EAT

Acapulco: As in all beach resorts, try the *ceviche* (marinated raw fish or shell-fish) and *delfín* steaks. Although *delfín* translates to "dolphin," this is not the TV darling species, but merely another saltwater fish.

Olinalá: You won't be able to get to this remote Guerrero pueblo, but look for the spectacular, inlaid-lacquer work of the village in Casa Humboldt in Taxco.

Taxco: The Easter week religious ceremonies are excessive in fervor but alluring to some. Silver, silver, silver is in abundance here, even though the prices for the same pieces are often less expensive in Mexico City. Take the cable car up to Monte Taxco for a margarita at sunset. The only regional specialty of the area is iguana, tasty but repulsive to Anglo palates, and not to be found on first-class menus.

Cuernavaca: For the art lovers and collectors, the Museo Brady and David Alfaro Siqueiros' Workshop are two priorities. Plan a drink and a tour of the grounds at the Ex-Hacienda Cortés. For perhaps the dining highlight of your trip, have luncheon or dinner in the spectacular garden and aviary at Las Mañanitas. (The curry, calves' brains, avocado soup, and ceviche are world class.)

Tepoztlán: This was the movie site for "The Good, the Bad, and the Ugly," "The Magnificent Seven," and others. Not much here but the beauty of the surrounding crags, the ghost of Tepozteco, the god of *pulque*,[1] and a sometimes interesting Sunday market.

Puebla: Hand-painted Mexican Talavera tile and pottery work, beautiful dinner-ware and serving pieces (expensive), and Museo Amparo and Museo Bello for the antique-buffs are all found here. Note the largely unappreciated 18th- and 19th-century Poblano marquetry furniture. Fine alabaster (Pueblan onyx) arti-facts, and fantastic **food**. Elsewhere in this chapter look for *Mole Poblano*, *Chalupas*, *Pipián Verde*, and unusual sweets.

Tlaxcala: "Blue" tortillas made from a coarse Indian corn are filled with spiced squash blossoms (see recipe page 98) are found here along with tacos of maguey worms, fried and spiced with salt and chili powder.

Toluca: The Friday market is the largest (and the most commercial) in Mexico. The rough, hand-knit sweaters made by the local Mazahuán and Matlatzincán women are good buys. Look for magnificent hand-carved chess sets in sizes

---

[1] Pulque is the raw, liquid heart of the maguey cactus. It is extracted through a long gourd called a tlachique and drunk straight or "curado" with fruit juice. It ferments immediately upon being drained from the cactus and continues to grow stronger with time.

from miniature to man-size. Be careful with a chess challenge, you may find your rebozo-ed Indian vendor is a chess master and invites you to a match for double or nothing. Handmade wooden kitchen utensils are useful and a conversation piece. Spicy *chorizo* is also made and sold.

Valle de Bravo: The faces of the aged Indians seated around the small plaza are an artist's dream come true. Look for a golden-brown glazed pottery indigenous to the town and rustic leather and wood furniture. The food is forgettable.

Mexico City: (See next chapter) Everything—the best of the best and the worst of the worst, an adventurers delight!

CEVICHE (CEBICHE)

Lime Pickled Fish

Serves 6

> *Acapulco stakes the oldest claim to this now international dish. Its variations are myriad. Some favorites are lobster, shrimp, and for easiest adaptation, I substitute bay or calico scallops for the fish. Don't eschew the dish because you're not a chile lover—it's delicious also without the intense "bite"—use a bit more lime juice or a little Balsamic vinegar.*

2 pounds firm fish fillets, cut into bite-sized pieces
juice of 6 lemons or 8–10 limes
1 large white onion, minced
2 medium-sized tomatoes, chopped fine
2 tablespoons olive oil
1/4 cup fresh cilantro/coriander, chopped
2 tablespoons parsley, chopped fine
1/2 teaspoon oregano
1/4 teaspoon thyme
15 stuffed olives, chopped
1 cup catsup
salt and pepper, to taste
2 Serrano chilies, or to taste, chopped and seeded
2 ripe avocados, peeled, pitted, and chunked

1. Place the fish (or other seafood) in a deep glass dish and completely cover with lemon or lime juice. Allow to marinate for an hour in the refrigerator, mixing gently several times.
2. Drain the fish and return to the glass bowl.
3. Combine the remaining ingredients in a small bowl and pour over the fish. Allow to marinate for several hours in the refrigerator. Pour off any excess liquid.
4. Serve in individual glass or pottery deep dishes, garnished with cilantro/coriander and avocado. Serve very cold with salted crackers.

SOPA DE AGUACATE

Avocado Soup

Serves 6

1 teaspoon chopped garlic
¼ cup fresh cilantro/
   coriander leaves
3 ripe avocadoes, peeled and
   pitted
1 teaspoon coarse salt
½ teaspoon freshly ground
   black pepper
1 teaspoon fresh lemon juice
½ cup heavy cream (optional:
   substitute
   ½ cup low-fat ricotta
   cheese)
4 cups chicken broth, every trace of fat removed
1 teaspoon Tabasco sauce, or to taste
½ cup chopped chives
6 sprigs fresh cilantro/coriander
½ pound tortilla chips

If ever there was a preview of Heaven on earth, the restaurant/inn, Las Mañanitas, in Cuernavaca would certainly qualify. How many lovers' (including this author), have whiled away a warm afternoon or evening in its paradisiac gardens, and then dined on a level with the world's best. Charming host/owner Rubén Cerdá, introduced us to this creamy, green soup, and this recipe is an adaptation of which I hope he would approve.

1. Purée the garlic and cilantro/coriander in the bowl of a food processor with a steel blade. Add the avocados, salt, pepper, and lemon juice. Process until completely smooth.

2. If using cream, whip until soft peaks hold, or purée the ricotta until smooth. In a large bowl, fold the avocado and cream or ricotta into the chicken broth. Season with Tabasco.

3. Transfer to individual serving bowls, sprinkle with the chopped chives, and garnish with cilantro/coriander. Refrigerate, covered, until ready to serve, but no more than 2 hours. Serve with tortilla chips in a basket on the side.

SOPA DE CEBOLLA TOLUQUEÑA

Toluca-style Onion Soup

Serves 4

1 tablespoon butter or
    margarine
1 tablespoon vegetable oil
2 cups chopped onions
2 cups milk
2 eggs yolks, beaten
2 cups boiling beef stock
salt and pepper, to taste
¼ cup Toluca or Gruyere-type
    cheese, fine-cubed

1. In a 3-quart, heavy-bottomed soup pot, heat the butter and oil together. Add the onions and brown until almost caramelized.
2. In a medium-sized saucepan, scald the milk and whisk in the egg yolks. Add to the onions, stirring constantly.
3. Heat the stock in a small saucepan, and when at a full boil, add to the onion mixture. Season to taste with salt and pepper. Serve topped with cheese cubes.

The Friday market in Toluca is mind boggling in its expanse. The vegetable section always draws me—I find myself cooking in my head: peeling ripe-red tomatoes, deciding which chili will be most savory in my imaginary dish, and always, always, chopping mounds of sweet, snowy white onions.

If you want this soup to be as sweet as it is in Mexico, use large, flattish white onions (the round ones are sharper), or the Sweet Texas or Vidalia strains.

CHISME

"BASTA"—WITH THE CHICKEN SOUP

In Spanish, *basta* is a tricky word. If used as the command form of the word *bastar*, it means "to suffice." You will find yourself saying *basta* when you mean you've had more than enough of something: a traffic tie-up, a third portion of dessert, or the sound of a kitchen full of squabbling *muchachas* or siblings.

The derivative, *bastante* has two, diametrically opposed meanings, and here's where it can get hairy.

Leaning over my cook's shoulder one morning, I asked for a spoonful of soup to taste for seasoning. Yecch!—it tasted like dishwater. How could all that chicken swimming around in that pot with fresh, green vegetables, orange carrots, and red, ripe tomatoes, taste so bland. Quick, the salt!

Concha wielded the shaker with a symphony conductor's delicacy. I tapped her shoulder indicating *more*; and she stepped up her shaking rhythm to a rapid quick step. She got so **much** into it, that I tapped her again and said, *Bastante*, meaning, of course, "that's enough." She slid me an exasperated glance and accelerated her *Cha-cha* with the salt cellar.

What a *mula*[1] . . . couldn't she understand Spanish? I started to shout **B A S T A N T E**, and she continued to pour salt.

Finally, desperately, I pried the offending seasoning out of her hand, and told her to throw the whole mess away . . . it was ruined! I stamped off to my bedroom and grabbed my dictionary to search for choice words with which to call "Cook" to account. The page fell open to *bastar*.

Oh, what shame, the great grammarian in the sky was really letting me have a taste of divine one-upsmanship. Mr. Webster really gave it to me.

The use of *basta* would have been fine in the "imperative" sense of the verb, as "that's enough!!!"

Bastante, used all by itself in the idiomatic sense, means: **use** enough; or use **plenty**. Now who was the *mula*?

---

[1] Stubborn one

MOLE POBLANO

Chili Sauce from Puebla

Yield: 6 cups

- 4 dried ancho chilies
- 4 dried mulato chilies
- 3 canned chipotle chilies
- 1 large tomato, peeled and cored
- 1 large onion
- 3 cloves garlic
- 5 tablespoons vegetable oil
- 1 tablespoon raisins
- 2 whole cloves
- 2 tablespoons sesame seeds, toasted
- 1 tablespoon peanut butter
- 1/2 teaspoon ground cinnamon
- pinch of cumin powder
- 4 level tablespoons unsweetened cocoa
- 4 cups chicken broth
- 3 stale French rolls or 1/2 small baguette, chunked

Here it is, the secret sauce (pro-nounced mow-lay), mentioned elsewhere in these pages as that "chocolate sauce." Now, you can go out to your nearest His-panic market and buy mole paste in jars, or little rectan-gular packages, and mix it with chicken broth, and instant "Chef" . . . but that wouldn't tell you what was in it, or how much work it is to do it from scratch.

Here is my "simplest" M.O. for one of the world's great culinary creations, using several shortcuts, and substi-tuting cocoa and vegetable oil for the artery-clogging chocolate and lard. If you promise not to tell anyone, I'll confess that I often start with the commercial product and then "doctor" to my taste.

1. Handle the dried chilies care-fully, as described on page 180. Remove the seeds and veins from the chipotle chilies. In a blender, purée all the chilies with the tomato, onion, and garlic. Sauté for 5 minutes to allow the flavors to meld. Set aside.
2. In a large, heavy skillet, heat the vegetable oil and sauté the raisins, cloves, sesame seeds, peanut butter, cinnamon, and cumin for about 5 minutes, stirring constantly to avoid burning.

3. Whisk the cocoa into the chicken broth stirring until it is incorporated. Drop in the bread chunks, stirring to moisten them.
4. Incorporate all 3 mixtures and process or grind into a smooth paste. Return to a low flame and cook for about 45 minutes. If the sauce gets too thick add more broth.
5. Pour over almost-cooked fowl (roasted or in a Dutch oven), cover, and continue cooking for another 15 minutes. Serve with *mole* basted over the bird and sprinkled with additional sesame seeds.

Note: Lots of hot tortillas are necessary here to make tacos or simply to soak up this ambrosial sauce. White rice is the usual accompaniment.

TORTA DE FLOR DE CALABAZA

Squash Blossom Fritters

Serves 4

As ubiquitous as are the members of the squash family, the population explosion of these hardy gourds is kept under control by the delicious use of their flowers. Elsewhere in these pages is a recipe for a fragrant, golden soup made with these blossoms; this however is my favorite.

24 squash blossoms
1 6-ounce package cream cheese, divided into 24 portions
2 tablespoons flour
3 eggs, separated
$1/2$–$3/4$ cup vegetable oil
3 large tomatoes, peeled and drained
2 tablespoons chili powder
1 medium-sized onion, chopped

1. Remove the stems and pistils from the squash blossoms. Wash well and cut in halves lengthwise.
2. Put 3 blossom halves on a work surface, then add a portion of cheese. Place 3 more on top and repeat with 3 more halves. Sprinkle with flour, making 6 of these "sandwiches."
3. Beat the egg whites, then separately beat the yolks. Fold together. Dip the flower sandwiches into the beaten eggs and quick-fry in hot oil. Remove from the oil, drain on paper towels, and keep hot in a low oven.
4. Sauté the remaining ingredients in the remaining oil until thoroughly limp.
5. Put the flower fritters on a hot platter. Pour the tomato/onion mixture over the fritters. Serve at once as an appetizer or side dish. Excellent with poultry or pork.

LOMO DE CERDO TALAVERANO

Pork Roast with Prune Sauce

Serves 6–8

2½ pounds pork tenderloin
4 tablespoons bacon fat or
  vegetable oil
1 medium-sized onion,
  chopped
1 large clove garlic, mashed
1 large tomato, peeled and
  chopped
½ pound pitted prunes,
  plumped in wine, juice, or water
2 teaspoons brown sugar
½ can chipotle chiles, drained, seeded, and halved
¼ teaspoon ground cloves
1 12-ounce bottle regular cola drink

Cooking with dried fruit is another legacy from those Spaniards who settled in Puebla, although versions of this savory recipe are served everywhere in Mexico. This is my version of a dish we first enjoyed in the Fonda Santa Clara, after a day of Talavera tile shopping in the famed Casa Ruggerio. I still serve this on the prized, oval serving platter I bought that day.

1. Rinse and thoroughly dry the pork loin.
2. In a large saucepan, heat 2 tablespoons of the fat or oil and lightly sauté the onion and garlic. Add the tomato, plumped prunes, sugar, chipotle chilies, and cloves, and simmer for 1–2 minutes. Set aside.
3. Put the remaining fat into a heavy skillet with a cover or a Dutch oven. Heat until the fat sizzles. Add the pork loin and sear on all sides, allowing to brown slightly.
4. Pour the sauce over pork and empty the cola around the loin, taking care not to wash off the sauce from the loin itself. Cover and simmer for about 40 minutes on top of the stove.
5. Heat the oven to 350°F. Uncover the pot, baste the loin, and roast in the oven for another 30 minutes or until the meat thermometer registers 170°F.

HUACHINANGO BANDERA MEXICANA

Mexican Flag Red Snapper

Serves 4

Because Pacific snappers can be much larger than the Gulf variety, you are often served fillets or steaks of the snowy fish. I first enjoyed this handsome dish in the Pierre Marqués Hotel in Acapulco. The colors of the Mexican flag are red, white, and green—hence the name of this presentation.

⅓ cup vegetable oil
1 pound mushrooms, sliced
    thin
1 cup chopped onions
4 red snapper steaks, cut 1-inch thick
4 medium-sized, ripe tomatoes, chopped (seeds and liquid
    strained out)
olive or vegetable oil
4 Jalapeño peppers, seeded, deveined, and julienned
4 medium-sized, unblemished mushrooms (for garnish)

1. Heat the oil and sauté the sliced mushrooms until lightly browned. Separately brown the onions and set aside.
2. Cut 3 diagonal slits in each steak, about 1-inch apart, taking care not to cut all the way through.
3. Fill the first slit with sautéed mushrooms, the second with the sautéed onions, and the third with the chopped tomatoes.
4. Brush the top of each steak with oil and put under the broiler for about 2 minutes. Lower the heat and continue cooking for no more than 3–4 minutes. Serve at once, garnished with the Jalapeño slices and the whole mushrooms.

ENSALADA CHARREADA

Tossed Salad, Charro-style

Serves 4

Vinaigrette:
½ cup olive oil
½ cup cider vinegar
2 cloves garlic, peeled and
    mashed
2 splashes of Maggi
1 teaspoon sugar
salt and pepper, to taste

Salad:
1 large head iceberg lettuce,
    crisped and shredded
1 large white onion, sliced
    in thin rounds
12 small ripe, peeled tomatoes,
    sliced thin
4 Jalapeño chilies, rinsed and
    seeded (may use canned)

The Charros are an exclusive group of gentlemen (and women) horse owners, trainers, and competitors. On Sunday mornings in Mexico City, dressed in priceless, silver-laden charro costumes, the Charro families (including straight-backed tots), parade their magnificent mounts up the Paseo de la Reforma. Each saddle is a triumph of the leather and silvermaster's artistry, and can cost as much as $50,000.

A Charreada is the cross between a rodeo and a bullfight, celebrated frequently by the national Society of Charros. It also entails a huge, colorful party with music, lots of tequila, and marvelous food. My first experience with being "enchilada" (struck speechless by the fire of a chile-laden dish) was at a Charreada at the Hacienda de Vista Hermosa in Morelos. I mistook slivers of chile huachinango (a particularly fiery local pepper) for slices of plum tomatoes—wow!

1. In a small bowl, whisk together the 6 ingredients of the vinaigrette. Set aside and allow to season while you prepare the salad.
2. Arrange the shredded lettuce on a serving platter or in a shallow salad bowl. Top with onion and tomato slices.
3. Slice the Jalapeño chilies into thin rounds or fine julienne and sprinkle over top of salad. Mix the vinaigrette well and drizzle over salad.

ACELGAS EN SALSA DE HUEVO

Swiss Chard with Golden Sauce

Serves 6

1 pound fresh Swiss chard
or spinach (1 package of
frozen, drained)
3 hard-cooked eggs
1 boiled potato, peeled and
diced
¼ cup olive oil
1 teaspoon wine vinegar
salt and pepper, to taste

1. Wash the fresh chard or spinach well and coarsely chop. Boil the fresh or frozen leaves in salted water for 5 minutes. Drain.
2. Mash the cooked eggs with a fork and toss with the potato, oil, vinegar, and salt and pepper. Blend the cooked chard or spinach with the egg mixture and serve at once.

Chard, both the red-veined and the white-veined variety, is a produce staple in Mexico. It is particularly savory served with the succulent pork of fresh markets, like that of Amecameca, which lies at the foot of the snow-capped volcano, Popocatépetl.

I remember when newly arrived in Mexico, I took my first trip to the pueblo with a new Mexican friend, Luisa. She asked me to stay in the car while she bargained, figuring that the price would be higher for her gringa companion. I suspect also, that she felt I wasn't yet ready for the sights and smells of a country market—she was wrong, I adored the whole experience! (P.S. I also quickly learned to haggle in appropriate Mexican Spanish. It's a game and both sides enjoy it!)

POLLO ALMENDRADO

Chicken with Almond Sauce

Serves 4

1 young chicken (2 pounds)
1 whole chicken breast,
  quartered
3 tablespoons flour
salt and pepper, to taste
3 tablespoons vegetable oil
3 tablespoons light olive oil
1 large onion, chopped
1 tablespoon paprika
2 tomatoes, skinned, seeded,
  and chopped
1 cup almonds, blanched, with skins slipped
1 pinch saffron (optional, but it gives a nice perfume)
¼ teaspoon ground cloves
1 small cinnamon stick or ¼ teaspoon ground cinnamon
4 cups chicken stock
1 pinch thyme
splash of almond liqueur, optional
mint or thyme sprig

Almond trees grow in profusion all along the Guerrero Coast, and when they are in bloom, their scent is intoxicating.

Chicken in Mexico is a luxury dish, the bird itself being more expensive than it is in the U.S. The exquisitely delicate almond sauce makes the dish a national favorite. Add a splash of almond liqueur right before serving, and smile like the Cheshire cat when the compliments come.

1. Singe and clean the chicken and cut into serving pieces. Sprinkle with flour and salt and pepper. Heat the oils in a large skillet and brown the chicken, turning several times.

2. Add the onion and paprika. When the onion is transparent, add the tomatoes. Cover and simmer until the chicken is tender, about 30 minutes.

3. In a small, heavy fry pan, heat a tiny amount of oil or oil spray and brown the almonds until golden, shaking the pan constantly. Grind in a miniprocessor with the saffron, cloves, and cinnamon until medium grainy. Return to the pan, add the stock and thyme, taste the sauce, and adjust the salt and pepper. Cover and simmer on very low heat. Add the optional liqueur.

4. Place the chicken in a heated casserole dish and pour the sauce over it. Serve with white rice and a green salad or vegetable. Garnish with mint or thyme sprig.

CHORIZO DE TOLUCA

Toluca Pork Sausage

Makes 2 pounds of sausage meat

3 ancho chiles
2 pasilla chiles[1]
1 teaspoon coriander/cilantro
  seeds
5 whole cloves
½ teaspoon black pepper
  corns
½ teaspoon cumin seed
1 teaspoon oregano
3 tablespoons paprika
2–3 teaspoons salt
1 teaspoon cinnamon
½ cup tequila
4 cloves garlic, mashed
½ cup vinegar (any variety)
2½ pounds boneless, lean
  pork (but with fat rind)

Taquear *means, to eat tacos—and tacos are most often eaten standing. All over the city of Toluca on market days, you will see (and smell) the wares of the taco vendors, flipping little chunks of the local, homemade sausage on their charcoal braziers. The vendors chase the spicy meat randomly with the side of their battered spatulas and scoop the fragrant morsels into hand-held warm tortillas. Writing about them I can recall that unequalled fragrance and begin to salivate. Warning: This is not healthy food, but it sure tastes great!*

1. To prepare the chilies, tear them into several flat pieces and heat them in a medium-sized iron skillet, pressing down with a spatula and turning each piece several times. You do not want them to burn, just to blister.

2. Cool the chilies, discard the seeds, and grind them in a mini-processor or spice grinder with the coriander/cilantro, cloves, pepper corns, cumin, and oregano.

---

[1] If you can't find both varieties, don't panic, settle for double the quantity of one.

3. Make a paste of the spices using the tequila, add the garlic and vinegar, cover, and let rest to allow flavors to meld while you work with the meat.
4. Grind or process the pork with the fat. Mix well with the tequila/spice paste, place in a colander, set over a large bowl to catch the drippings. Cover, and refrigerate for 2 days.
5. Follow the instructions that come with the sausage casings (usually packed in salt). Before filling the casings, fry a bit of the mixture and add salt if needed. Each finished link should be about 5 inches long.

or

Make patties and freeze them between sheets of waxed paper, wrapped well in aluminum foil or freezer plastic wrap for use up to 6 months. In most appreciative families they don't last longer than a few days.

ROPA VIEJA[1]

Shredded Meat

Serves 4–6

Mexican beef often is tough and chews as if the steer had fast-jogged the thousand plus miles to the border. This is a wonderful summer salad that allows you to cook a less expensive cut of beef with gourmet results. If you're feeling splendid, use flank or skirt steak, the flavor is great!

2 tablespoons vegetable oil
1 pound beef steak
1/2 medium-sized onion, minced
2 cloves garlic, minced or mashed
3 carrots
bunch parsley
4 whole cloves
1 teaspoon chili sauce or powder (optional)
2 medium-sized tomatoes, quartered
6 radishes, sliced in rounds
1 sweet onion, sliced thin
1 avocado, peeled and sliced
1/2 cup good vinaigrette
salt and pepper, to taste
fresh coriander/cilantro as garnish

1. Heat the oil in a Dutch oven or heavy pan with a cover and sear the meat. Cover with the beef stock and add the onion, garlic, carrots, parsley, and cloves, and allow to cook until the meat is so tender it falls apart.
2. Shred the meat and return to the stock to cool. Drain, discard the vegetables, and reserve the stock for future use.
3. In a large salad bowl, mix the shredded meat with the chili sauce (or powder), tomatoes, radishes, onion, and avocado. Toss lightly with the vinaigrette. Chill. Garnish with coriander/cilantro sprigs and serve.

We always serve this with hot quesadillas (see page 74).

---

[1] Translation: Old clothes

ALBONDIGÓN RELLENO

Stuffed Meat Loaf

Serves 6

3 small French rolls, torn
   into pieces
½ cup milk
1 pound of lean ground beef
1 pound ground turkey
2 large eggs, beaten
1 medium-sized onion, grated
2 cloves garlic, mashed
1 teaspoon dried oregano
1 teaspoon ground cumin
½ teaspoon cinnamon
1 teaspoon salt
3 hard-cooked eggs
1 small jar of strips of
   pimiento (for garnish)
catsup

Meat loaf is as international as meatballs (indeed Albondigón translates to "big meatball")—and as the versions vary from country to country so do they from region to region in a country that worships ground beef.

In the impressive Mexico the Beautiful Cookbook, Susanna Palazuelos offers a version from San Luís Potosí that is filled with red and green chilies. This recipe is a common variation found in the central part of Mexico and taught me by gentle Regina Martínez, from Puebla. The use of ground turkey, to substitute the orginal ground pork, is my own bow to lower fat cookery.

1. Soak the torn bread in the milk until all the liquid is absorbed.
2. Blend all of the ingredients except the eggs, mixing well with your hands (there's no better way to do this).
3. Preheat the oven to 350°F. Grease a 4 x 8 x 4-inch loaf pan and lay in half of the meat mixture. Smooth with a spatula without compressing (it makes the loaf tough).
4. Lay the peeled eggs in a line down the middle and cover with the rest of the meat mixture. Brush with catsup and bake for about 50 minutes.

CLEMOLE CON SALSA DE RÁBANOS

. . . .

Pork and Vegetable Stew with Radish Sauce

Serves 6

Soup:
1½ pounds boneless lean pork, cubed
½ onion
3 cloves garlic
10 cups water
2 tablespoons salt
1½ pounds *tomatillos*, husks removed
1 cup chopped fresh coriander/cilantro (3 teaspoons dried)
3 chiles serranos
3 ears corn, each cut into 3 pieces
3 small zucchini, sliced ½-inch thick
½ pound green beans, trimmed and cut in half

Sauce:
1 cup water
1 tablespoon salt
1 tablespoon vinegar (any variety)
4 Poblano chiles, roasted, peeled, membranes removed, and cut into strips
6 radishes, finely chopped
½ cup finely chopped onion
¾ cup orange juice
½ cup lime juice

This soupy stew from Puebla, might well be the area's own version of Pozole (see page 78). As with many Mexican recipes, this has numerous ingredients, but their blending really is not time consuming—into the pot with all of it while you prepare the sauce. Once you get the hang of dealing with dried chilies, they really are not that much work, and oh, how good they make the kitchen smell!

1. Place the pork, onion, garlic, water, and salt in a large pot or Dutch oven. Bring to a boil, skim the surface, reduce the heat, and simmer, covered, until the pork is tender, about 45 minutes.
2. In a blender, purée the tomatillos, cilantro, and chiles serranos. Set aside.
3. To make the sauce, combine the water, salt, and vinegar in a bowl, add the chiles Poblanos and soak for 30 minutes. Drain the chiles and combine with the radishes, onion, orange juice, and lime juice.
4. Twenty minutes before serving, bring the pork mixture to a boil, add the corn, zucchini, and green beans, and simmer until the vegetables are tender, 10–15 minutes. Bring the soup to a boil, add the tomatillo purée, stir, and remove from the heat.

Pass the sauce separately, to be served over the hot soup. Serve with good bread—French-type hard rolls are customary in Mexico— you must have something handy to sop up the last few spoonfuls.

ADOBO

Spicy Seasoning Rub

Serves 4; Yield: 1+ cups

8 medium-sized ancho chilies
  (pasilla or guajillos can
  be substituted)
1/2 cup red wine
5 cloves garlic, peeled and
  mashed
good pinch ground cloves
3 tablespoons wine vinegar
1/4 teaspoon oregano
1/4 teaspoon cumin seeds
1/4 teaspoon dried thyme
1-inch cinnamon stick or 1/2 teaspoon ground
6–8 whole black peppercorns

The name Adobo *comes from the verb "adobar" which means to pickle. It is the naughty first cousin to a* Recado *(see page 260), naughty in that it contains one or several kinds of chili. Both mixtures are used as dry rubs or mixed with juice, liquor, or broth to form a kind of marinade which later converts to a liquid sauce for stewing.*

1. Prepare the chilies as described on page 173. Still wearing gloves, tear the chilies into pieces and place them in the glass jar of a blender.
2. In a small saucepan, simmer the garlic cloves for 5 minutes in the red wine. Reserve half the wine and add the remaining wine and garlic to the blender. Add the cloves and the vinegar to the blender.
3. With the blender on its slowest speed or pulsing on and off, add all of the remaining spices, little by little. Take your time, pulsing and scraping down the sides of the jar.

Note: If the paste is unmanageably thick, add a little of the reserved wine in which the garlic was simmered. Blend until smooth. Adobo will keep in the refrigerator for up to a week in a glass jar.

Use as a seasoning rub or marinade with poultry or meat.

ENSALADA DE CHAYOTES

Spiny Squash Salad

Serves 6

Chayotes are a member of the squash family, but in Mexican garb—that is, they wear a spiny coat, like a cactus. Their flavor is bland, making a perfect foil for savory stuffings or this unusual salad. Because I was first introduced to this versatile vegetable in the Tepoztlán home of friends, I'll include it in this section, although it is enjoyed everywhere.

4 chayotes (sometimes called vegetable pears)
1 large clove garlic, minced
8 tablespoons light olive oil
4 tablespoons wine vinegar
salt and pepper, to taste
1 teaspoon juice from capers
1 sweet red pepper, chopped
3 tablespoons fresh coriander/cilantro, chopped
4 scallions, chopped with ½ the green tops
1 tablespoon capers (for garnish)

1. In a large saucepan, cook the chayotes with water to barely cover until tender when pierced with a fork. Do not overcook or they become mushy. Drain, and when cool enough to handle, peel.
2. In a small bowl, whisk together the garlic, oil, vinegar, salt and pepper, and caper juice to make a vinaigrette.
3. Chop the chayote into bite-sized pieces, toss with the red pepper, coriander/cilantro, and scallions. Pour the vinaigrette on top and toss again. Allow to season in the refrigerator for an hour or two. Serve topped with the capers.

RITUAL
FOR THE
PREPARATION
OF A CURATIVE
TAMALE

Translated from La Comida en el México Antiquo y Moderno, *by Virginia Rodriguez Rivera (Editorial Pormaca, S.A.de C. V. 1961)*

Leafing through a tattered little book my eldest son had picked up in a bookstall in Mexico City, I came across this recipe for a tamale to cure a hex. Reproduce at your peril!

Tapataxtle: The ritual "to crush an evil or sickness," comes from the area of the Huejutla ranches in the Huasteca region of Hidalgo. It was reported by Dr. Germán Fernández Arámburu from Puebla.

. . . It is a tamale measuring seventy-five centimeters in length. It is made for magic-therapy; the treatment is carried out by a *brujo* (medicine man), specialist in the curing of patients who are ill due to bewitching.

Coinciding with the sex of the patient, a rooster or hen will be sacrificed . . . with the patient lying down, a cleansing is made with the fowl, holding it by its wings and feet. At this time the prayers: Our Father is said once, the Ave María once and three "Credos," generally in Náhuatl.[1] After this the bird is tied in a corner of the room while the *brujo* prepares the tamal.

The fowl is taken from the room well covered with a dark cloth, because the malevolent cause of the patient's ill is now in the bird. It (the bird) is washed well, and the innards removed. Quickly dredge chile colorado over the middle of the cavity and place it in the middle of the tamale dough, on top of flattened banana leaves. The bird must remain in one piece. Wrap the dough around and then the leaves, and tie the tamal. It must be cooked in a very large casserole called a *Chichapal*.[2]

Once the tamal is cooked put it in the middle of the sick room and surround it with seven wax candles, a bottle of *aguardiente* and a jar of water. Open the leaves, slice the tamal, and have everyone present eat, first the family and then the visitors. Everyone should drink some *aguardiente* and some water, being careful to leave the bones and scraps of the fowl on the same banana leaves in which it was cooked. Finally make a package with the remains. The *brujo* should then take it as far as possible from the patient's house and bury it saying:

I deliver here this cleansing so that you return the patient to me and release him. Here is your payment. This favor is asked of the brujo of the earth and the four winds.

Sometimes it is said:

I deliver here this cleansing to the winds for the relief of (patient's name).

---

[1] Náhuatl is the tongue of the ancient Aztecs, it is still widely spoken today.
[2] Dialect for a "meat cooker."

CAPIROTADA CUARESMEÑA DE TAXCO

Lenten Bread Pudding

Serves 6

2 cups milk
½ cup dark Karo corn syrup (molasses may be substituted)
1 stick cinnamon
1 cup white raisins
1 slightly stale French baguette, or 6 French hard rolls[1]
½ stick (⅛ pound) sweet butter
4 tortillas, toasted
1 cup peanuts or pine nuts
½ cup *queso añejo* (Feta cheese works well here)

1. In a medium-sized saucepan, bring the milk, corn syrup, cinnamon stick, and raisins to a simmer. Allow the flavors to meld for 2 minutes, then remove from the stove to cool.
2. Slice the bread or rolls into ½-inch thick rounds. Spread each slice with butter.

Taxco has long been the eye of the tourist hurricane. There are so many things to see and do and buy! But the alma (soul) of the city truly bares itself during Holy Week, the week prior to Easter, when observances blending pagan and Christian are celebrated.

On Good Friday, the altars to Our Lady of Sorrows are lavishly decorated, and all statues of the Holy Virgin are dressed in mourning purple and black. In the famed church of Santa Prisca, the somberly-clad parishioners contrast sharply with the churrieresque excess of gold leaf. Soberly baroque on the outside, the interior of the church explodes into a combination of glitter, color, and naif-religious tableaux. (The high altar with its 32 popes peeking from biblical symbols is worth the visit alone.)

This rich bread pudding is a traditional Lenten dessert, made by cooks everywhere with their own loving variations—this is a favorite of mine, given to me by one of the elderly cooks from the Hotel Victoria in Taxco.

---

[1] It's important that the bread or rolls are not too stale or you'll be unable to slice them. If you prefer, use fresh bread, slice, and then dry it out on a cookie sheet in the oven.

3. Heat the oven to 350°F. Grease a square, 9-inch, oven-proof casserole.

4. Line the greased casserole with the toasted tortillas. Top with 1 layer of buttered bread. Sprinkle with the nuts and crumbled cheese. Slowly cover with half of the milk mixture. Repeat for a second layer. Drizzle additional corn syrup or molasses over the top.

5. Cover the casserole with aluminum foil and bake for 20 minutes. Uncover, and continue to bake until the top is nicely browned. Serve warm.

FLAN DE ALMENDRAS

Almond Custard

Serves 6

1 cup water
1 can sweetened *condensed*
  milk
1 cup almonds, blanched,
  toasted, and ground fine
2 egg whites, beaten medium-
  stiff
4 large egg yolks, beaten lightly
2 tablespoons sugar
1/3 cup whole almonds, blanched

The origins of "flan" are 100 percent Old World Spanish, but because the creamy dessert appears on every menu in every restaurant in the Republic, it has come to be considered Mexico's national dessert. This is a quick, rich version. Elsewhere in these pages you will find a fruit-flavored flan (see page 218).

1. Bring the water to a boil in a small saucepan. Add the condensed milk and ground almonds and simmer for 3 minutes. Transfer to a large bowl and cool.
2. In a small bowl, slowly fold the egg whites into the yolks and add to the milk mixture, stirring constantly.
3. Put the sugar in a baking dish and heat until the sugar is caramelized. Rotate the dish, working very carefully, to coat the inner surface. Allow to cool slightly.
4. Fill the dish with the custard, place in a pan of water, and bake in a slow oven (325°F) for 30 minutes or until a knife inserted in the center comes out clean. Allow to cool and invert over a serving platter, heating the bottom of the flan to release it. Serve garnished with whole almonds.

DISTRITO FEDERAL

MEXICO CITY, THE CAPITAL

Mexico City, or the "D.F.," as it is sometimes called, deserves a chapter—no, a book, all her own! Sophisticated, bustling, and multilingual—(most educated Mexicans speak English and French as well as their own mellifluous tongue). In many places *Náhuatl*, the ancient language of the Aztecs, is still widely spoken by the indigenous population.

Mexico City, now the most populous city in the world, is a center of contrasts—great wealth and devastating poverty; beautiful gardens and choking air pollution; a fascinating growing middle class and noise— it is probably the noisiest city on the planet!

It is in the broad avenues of this megalopolis, as well as in the twisting pavements and cobbles of her suburbs, that gracious dining is a practiced art. International cuisine is the norm, blended with special touches that the products of the many native markets supply. Chefs and cooks from the entire ethnic spectrum have come over the years to practice their wizardry, free from preconceived culinary rules and morés. One can eat like royalty in her hundreds of premier restaurants.

If the same royalty is game to adventure, don jeans and tuck wallets securely away, there's a whole other epicurean experience to be savored. Public markets are found in every *barrio* (neighborhood), and somewhere on the premises there will be a homely counter or a grouping of metal card tables emblazoned with Corona Beer or Coca Cola logos. The chairs or stools will be odd fellows, but the food, bubbling or sizzling in front of you, over the braziers and in the *cazuelas* (clay casseroles), will be a gourmet revelation! If you're squeamish about offal meats or greens with which you're not familiar, don't partake, but do go and inhale at the very least—this is the true Mexican table!

Sundays in the Capital mean dining out. Mexican families take to their cars—expensive, clean, and shiny if they're upper class—and *carcachas* (tin lizzies held together with wire, chewing gum, and Hail Marys) if they're working class and lucky. Tlalpam and other outer suburbs are the destination, where rustic outdoor restaurants serve *carnitas* (pork loin seasoned and twice-cooked), *chicharrón* (crispy pork skin), *mixiotes* (pork, lamb, or pigeon, pit-baked in maguey leaves), and a dozen, lip-smacking side dishes, chased by fine Mexican beer or tequila.

For all this great city's sophistication there is always the whisper of danger, at once alluring and stimulating. Never does the traveler ever feel that he is anywhere but a foreign country ... it is a delicious feeling however, and appetite provoking. Try it, you may like it—*buen provecho!*

THINGS TO SEE, DO, AND EAT

MARKETS

La Merced: Rather than a single market, the Merced is a maze of many small markets, including the wholesale food purveying facilities that feed the vast city. There are individual small markets which are part of the complex, the straw market, and the candy market (*El Antiquo Mercado de las Dulces*), contained in an old church contiguous to the flower section of the main market.

Sonora: One of the most fascinating but least tourist-attended, this is also known as the *curanderos* (witches) market. There are two full aisles of potions, powders, and barrels of dessicated critters used in benevolent and malevolent witchcraft. Also known for its toys, cooking herbs, and everday cooking pottery.

San Juan: Food, flowers, and baskets are everywhere. Due to its accessibility to tourist paths, San Juan is extremely "sanitized" and also more expensive than other markets. I find it contrived.

Hidalgo: If you have a do-it-yourselfer traveling with you, this is the tool and plumbers' market. Any part of any piece of machinery made in the past 100 years can be found in the rubble-like stands. It's also a wonderful place to match tiles, or to buy beautiful old European tiles that have been bought from the demolition folk.

La Lagunilla: May be the largest and one of the oldest flea markets in the world—it has everything including great old book treasures and all manner of antiques (new and old)! Sundays only—but watch your wallet and your purse.

Bazar Sábado: This is really not a market, rather a gathering of craftsmen. It is located in a lovely old building with a flower-filled patio and a tinkling fountain. This is a fun place to spend Saturday morning through lunch. Don't neglect the open air vendors who set up all around. Wear comfortable shoes—the cobbled streets of San Angel are treacherous underfoot.

MUSEUMS

Mexico City is filled with museums to suit every taste. I must suggest that you refer to a guide book specifically for the city. An excellent one I have recommended elsewhere in this book is the *Cadogan Guides, Mexico*, Katherine and Charlotte Thompson.

If it's art you want, the city is a mother lode of creativity. Each Mexican child learns his history via the murals that beautify the walls of every public place. A "must see" is the Secretaría de Educación Pública, and the powerful

Polyforo of David Alfaro Siqueiros (he called it the Sistine Chapel of Mexico). The National Palace, Chapultepec Castle are all worth the trip. The school of Colonial art is seen everywhere, but for an extraordinary overview, the Museo Nacional de Arte is off the beaten path and seldom visited.

Don't miss the Tamayo Museum and the Museo de Arte Contemporáneo in Chapultepec Park, El Palacio Nacional de Bellas Artes near the Alameda, the Anahuacalli (Diego Rivera's studio), and the Frida Kahlo Museum in the south of the city.

I'VE SAVED THE BEST FOR LAST

I highly recommend the excavated Templo Mayor in (actually, *under*) the main zócalo, and the mind-boggling Museo Nacional de Antropología in Chapultepec Park. I've separated the other two museums and the castle, which are also in the park, because the Arthropology Museum deserves the better part of a day by itself, as does the Templo Mayor downtown.

SHOPPING

Before you riffle those traveler's checks see "How to Shop in a Mexican Market," page 14). Good buys are:

Silver—(look for the weight mark and the word "sterling"), and shop in upscale, transited areas (Plaza Polanco and La Rosa, for example). Sanborn's and Tané are good bets.

Leather goods at all levels are a buy, from belts to coats and hand-bags—top of the line, Aries and Gaitán.

Crafts—shop at the five FONART stores. They are government-run and the prices are the best. They will also pack and ship for you.

Clothing—Hand-embroidered, high-style, resort clothing, Girasol.

Gold jewelry can also be a buy, but shop in solid-looking stores in good neighborhoods. For the best—Flato and Villaumé.

Art—from inexpensive graphics to easel paintings of the Mexican greats. If you want big-eyed Mexican children on canvas, shop in the street markets, if you're a serious collector, go to Juan Martín, or to one of the large, long-established galleries like Misrachi.

Wrought iron—everything from tableware to lamps—Feder's (two locations).

DINING

Expensive—Hacienda de los Morales, San Angel Inn, Villa Reforma (fabulous Sunday brunch), **Les Célébritées, Isadora, Los Irabien**—all with a combination "Nouvelle Mexicaine" cuisine and the whim of the chefs. Reservations and jackets and ties, please.

Typically Mexican: Fonda el Refugio, Café Tacuba, Las Cazuelas, Las Palomas (take someone with you who speaks Spanish for all but the first). **Don Chon,** near the Zócalo, is the place for the adventurous eater. Specialties of the house reflect pre-Hispanic menus, including things that used to slither and hop.

Moderate: (German–Mexican) **Bellinghausen**. House specialties are the Osso Bucco, mushroom soup, langostinos, and chicken livers; **Lincoln** for fish (order the *Fuente de Mariscos*, Seafood Fountain). **El Arollo**, a Mexican "ranch" restaurant complete with its own bullring—fun! **La Góndola** (Italian), the Spaghetti Carbonara is a winner and the **Filete Siciliano** (see page 148), is also a good choice.

Cheap but wonderful: Beatriz (there are several of these throughout the city); **Panchos** near Chapultepec park—the best tacos in the world; and *Huevos Rancheros* or *Enchiladas Suizas* at any **Sanborn**'s.

EL MERCADO EN TENOCHTITLÁN

The Market, Aztec-style

The art of multiservice merchandising has been with us for a very long time. The East and the Middle East have been the site of vast selling bazaars since Biblical times. On our own continent, our neighbor Mexico refined the concept in pre-Columbian times.

The largest of the native markets, **Tlaltelolco,** was a place of wonder as reported by historians. Hernán Cortés wrote his monarch, Carlos V, a glowing description of the scope of wares offered for sale.

Cortés compared the size of the market to the Spanish city of Salamanca, and estimated that some 60,000 persons could be found buying and trading there on *Los Diás de Plaza* (market days). You would assume the offerings were of local manufacture and harvest, but Cortés raved that "everything found anywhere else on earth, could be found in Tlaltelolco."[1]

All kinds of edibles and staples were offered, but also a dizzying array of gold and silver jewelry; lead, bronze, copper, and tin objects; tools and implements made of bone, stones, shells, and feathers. Chunks of calcium were piled high waiting to be taken home and pulverized (calcium is an essential ingredient for the Mexican "staff of life," the tortilla), carved and quarry stone, bricks and wood (the wood in natural or already decoratively carved form).

Merchandising was divided into areas, a custom that is today common in Latin American cities. One entire alley was devoted to the sale of poultry, both wild and domesticated. Chicken, ducks, and turkeys of course, but also quail, pigeons, wild ducks, fly catchers, parrots, eagles, hawks, and even some buzzards. This inventory was live and noisy, straining at the cords which held them close to the seller.

Nearby, preserved vulture skins with feathers and claws intact, as well as enormous sacks of multi-colored feathers, were available for certain artisanry and the making of ceremonial headresses and garments.

Another area of stalls was dedicated to small game such as rabbit, hares, pygmy deer, and specially bred dogs (castrated young to render their meat more tender), called *Xoloesquintles.* Abutting this alley was the vast area of herb sellers.

Every leaf and root known to man at the time was for sale. These ancestors of today's "pitchmen" kept a running monologue going, extolling the curative virtues of each packet; detailing the guaranteed improvement of one's love life or the probable appeasing of the God who sent locusts to plague the farmers.

Interestingly the closest neighbors to the herbalists (*curanderos*) were the barbers, where Aztec gentlemen had their heads shaven and their topknots styled. (Wonder what they charged in those days . . . four ears of corn or a handful of sidewinder rattles . . . barter was the order of the day, of course!)

The vegetables that Hernán reported were artichokes, garlic, onions, nasturtium flowers, watercress, sorrel,

Confirmed by the chronicles of Bernal Díaz del Castillo[2] of Hernan Cortés' staff and the translations of Sahagún, we can marvel today at the advanced civilization of Mexico's indigenous forebearers. Barbarous religious rituals to the contrary, these speakers of *Náhuatl* (the Aztec tongue) adhered to rigid rules of citizen conduct, and even the elegance of their table manners was documented by the Spanish scribes. We can safely say that the Aztecs had refined palates and used condiments correctly, their tastes being comparable to that of the world's most respected gastronomes. They appreciated beauty in all things, commencing "at table."

---

[1] Translation of the Florentine Codices: Fray Bernardino de Sahagun.
[2] Chapter XCI *Historia de la Conquita de Neuva Espana.*

SOPA DE HUITLACOCHE[1]

Black Velvet Soup

Serves 4–6

2 tablespoons vegetable oil
½ pound or 1 8-ounce can *huitlacoche*
½ cup onion, minced
1 clove garlic, mashed
2 tablespoons *epazote*, dried, or substitute coriander/cilantro (see "Herbs and Spices" page 26)
2 cups sweet corn kernels (frozen or canned), drained
1 teaspoon Tabasco or other hot sauce (optional)
6 cups chicken broth
1 cup crème fraîche or light sour cream
salt and pepper, to taste

1. Heat the vegetable oil in a heavy 2–3 quart saucepan. Sauté the *huitlacoche* with the onion and garlic until the onion is transparent. Stir in the *epazote*, 1 cup of the corn kernels, and the Tabasco.

2. Heat and add the chicken broth and allow to simmer, covered, for 5 minutes to allow the flavors to meld. Purée the soup in a blender or processor until smooth Return to the pot and bring to a simmer. Add the second cup of corn kernels and stir in the crème fraîche just before serving. Serve with toasted tortilla wedges.

Before I begin, I must warn you that I've taken author's license to translate the name of this soup. Huitlacoche[1] in English is "corn smut," an unattractive name for an unattractive fungus that grows on corn ears, and has been considered a blight in the United States.[2]

However, forgive its appearance, for far from being a blight, it really is the truffle of Latin America, and quite as delicious. The corn growth is most often used in crepes and tacos, but this heavenly soup demonstrates its versatility.

Due to a greater demand for exotic foods by creative young chefs, there are several experimental produce farmers in the U.S. now marketing the precious fungus. The cooked black, corn growth has a velvety texture, hence my name.

---

[1] Also spelled *Cuitlacoche*.
[2] The translation of the Aztec word is even less appetizing, "excrement of the Gods."

CALDO XÓCHITL

. . . .

Chicken Soup Xóchitl

Serves 6

1 large stewing chicken (about
  4 pounds)
3–4 quarts water
½ teaspoon pickling spices
  (tied into cheesecloth bag)
6 cloves garlic, unpeeled
3 whole carrots
4 large outside stalks of celery,
  with leaves
1 sprig fresh parsley or herb of
  choice[2]
pinch sugar
2 cups white rice, cooked
6 fresh sage leaves
1 avocado, peeled and thinly sliced
½ white onion, diced
freshly ground black pepper
6 lemon wedges

> While travelling through
> Mexico as a journalist, I found
> that each of the over 200 indi-
> genous groups had their own
> version of this steaming elixir
> . . . a wild duck, a tropical bird,
> or an unlucky (but tasty)
> iguana may have substituted
> for our beloved hen, but the base
> ingredients were the same. Here
> is a Tlaxcalan cook's version
> named after Móctezuma's[1]
> beauteous daughter.

1. Wash the chicken and cut into serving pieces. Place in large
   stockpot with the water, pickling spices, garlic cloves, and salt.
   Allow to boil for about 40 minutes. Remove from the flame,
   cool, and skim off the fat.
2. Add the leeks, yellow onion, carrots, celery with leaves, parsley or herb of choice, and sugar. Simmer until the chicken is
   tender, about 15–20 minutes. Allow the soup to cool, and skim
   again.

---

[1] Sometimes spelled *Móntezuma*.
[2] As we use "dill" in Anglo and European countries, the Mexicans will substitute even more pungent
   herbs. In the southeast (Oaxaca and the Yucatán) "mint" will be used in place of parsley, and throughout most of the rest of the Republic, fresh coriander/cilantro leaves, make a nice counterpoint to the
   velvety texture of the avocado. Lemon wedges are always served on the side.

3. Remove all the vegetables from the broth, reserving only the garlic cloves and the carrots (which should be chopped and set aside).

4. Debone the chicken, cut into bite-sized chunks, and divide evenly between the serving mugs. To each mug, add a garlic clove, a teaspoon of chopped carrots, and a serving of rice.

5. Garnish with a bruised[3] sage leaf, a slice of avocado, a sprinkling of chopped onion wedges on the side, and a twist of freshly ground black pepper. Serve with lemon.

---

[3] "Bruising" releases the essential oils of the herbs. This can be done by rubbing the leaves between the palms of your hands.

SOPA DE FLOR DE CALABAZA

Mexican Squash Flower Soup

Serves 6

20 large squash flowers
4 cups well-seasoned chicken
   broth, all fat removed
2 medium-sized tomatoes,
   peeled
½ small onion, minced
3 tablespoons butter or margarine
½ teaspoon turmeric
Tabasco, to taste
sprig of parsley or *epazote* (see "Herbs and Spices" page 26)

Optional additions: (see note below)
1½ cups cooked zucchini, chopped
⅔ cup crème fraîche

There is no more spectacular sight than vast, golden fields of squash plants in flower. On your way to Xochimilco—the floating gardens—look to your right and left—you may be fortunate enough to catch the blooming season. Farmers carefully take only the male blossoms for market, leaving the females to mature and assure a bountiful squash crop.

1. Wash the flowers gently and remove the thick outer leaves, stems, and sepals. Chop coarsely. Place in a large saucepan with the broth and allow to simmer for about 15 minutes.
2. Skin the tomatoes by cutting out the stem scar, then dropping them into boiling water for 90 seconds. Chop coarsely. Sauté the tomatoes and onion in melted butter in a small sauté pan.
3. Mix the flowers in broth with the sautéed tomatoes and onion, simmering the mixture for 15 minutes, covered. Allow to cool slightly, and purée in blender.
4. Season with turmeric and a dash of Tabasco. Serve hot or cold, garnished with a sprig of parsley or *epazote*.

Note: To stretch the soup to serve 8 to 10, or to add more texture to the soup, add the cooked zucchini and top with crème fraîche.

MACARRÓN ENCHILADO

Chili-Spiced Macaroni

Serves 6

You haven't found many recipes for pasta in these pages, even though it is, along with rice, a familiar dish on Mexican tables. Its variety is limited however. You will find it prepared this spicy way and in a Sopa Aguada (see page 64). Because rice is the star in Mexico, the many charms of the wheat-based pasta have not yet been explored.

2 cups elbow macaroni
1 onion, chopped
2 tablespoons bacon fat or
   vegetable oil
1½ teaspoons salt
1 Jalapeño chili, peeled, seeded
   and chopped
2 cups stewed tomatoes,
   chopped
½ cup white Cheddar cheese, grated
pepper, to taste

1. Cook the macaroni according to the package directions until tender, and drain.
2. In a medium–sized skillet, heat the fat or oil, and sauté the onion. Add the salt, chili, and tomato, and mix with the macaroni.
3. Place the mixture in a buttered baking dish, cover with grated cheese, and bake slowly in a 325°F oven until the cheese is brown or about 25 minutes.

ARROZ BLANCA A LA MEXICANA

Mexican White Rice

Serves 4

1 cup long grain *raw* rice
1/2 cup vegetable oil
1/2 onion, chopped coarsely
1 garlic clove, peeled and
   bruised
1/2 teaspoon salt
2 cups chicken broth
1 tablespoon lemon juice (keeps the rice white)
1/4 teaspoon ground cumin (optional)

One of the "big three" of Mexican cuisine (beans, rice, and tortillas), the variations are limited only by the cook's imagination. Here is the base— now add your own signature; nuts, raisins, diced vegetables (confetti rice), fresh fruit cubelets . . . above all, your enthusiasm.

1. Put the rice in a sieve and rinse quickly under warm tap water. Drain well.
2. In a large pan with a tight-fitting cover, heat the oil and sauté the onion and garlic until transparent.
3. Add the rice and sauté lightly, stirring the rice continuously with a wooden spoon until it is a light golden color. (This seals the kernels so that each will be separate and flavorful.)
4. In a small saucepan, heat the broth to a boil. Add to the rice with the lemon juice and cumin all at once (it will sizzle wildly so step back a bit), stir several turns, cover tightly, bring to a rolling boil, then lower the heat to a mere "nothing." Low simmer for exactly 20 minutes—don't peek. If the rice has not absorbed all the liquid, cover, and allow to cook for another 3–5 minutes. Fluff with a fork before serving.

Note: To make Mexican Red Rice, substitute tomato juice for the broth.

FRIJOLES NEGROS

Black Beans

Serves 4

1 pound black beans
water
1 cup dry red wine
¼ teaspoon lemon zest
1 sprig *epazote* (optional) (see
   "Herbs and Spices" page 26)

1. Soak the beans overnight in cold water to cover. Discard any beans that float.
2. Drain and transfer the beans to a heavy saucepan and cover with cold water.
3. Simmer, covered, for 1–1½ hours, stirring from time to time.
4. Add the wine and zest (and *epazote*), and continue to simmer (1–1½ hours) until the beans are tender. Reserve the cooking liquid.
5. To make Mexican Black Rice, substitute the rsserved bean-cooking liquid for broth in the white rice recipe.

Black pasta is a darling of the "in" crowd—however, its strong, fishy flavor, derived from squid ink, is not to everyone's taste. Mexican black rice has that same deep hue but derives its color from a deliciously vegetarian source . . . black beans.

Follow the "how to" for Mexican White Rice (see page 132) but substitute the liquid left after you've cooked these nutritious black beans for the broth in the recipe on page 124.

LAS FLORES DE MÓCTEZUMA

More "edibles" trivia—flowers which are recent editions to our "nouvelle" and exotic cuisine here, were served at Móctezuma's court and formed part of the normal produce inventory of the time. Nasturtiums, marigolds, roses, and hibiscus blossoms-graced salads were consumed along with more ordinary vegetables, or steeped and drunk as teas—both for pleasure and curative purposes. Today's Mexican shares with the Italian, a predilection for squash flower fritters and soups; hibiscus tea and an infusion of magnolia blossoms is considered both salutary and aphrodisiac.

A visit to Mexico City's *Mercado de Sonora*, the witches' market, fascinates with barrels filled with dried and fresh herbs, as well as a sneeze-provoking selection of dried flowers and other unesthetic items for uses both culinary and mystical. This is a market I never miss.

GARBANZOS SAN ANGEL

Mexican Chickpea Casserole

Serves 4

3 slices lean bacon
1 tablespoon vegetable oil
2 tablespoons chopped onion
1 clove garlic, chopped
1 14-ounce can stewed
   tomatoes, chopped
½ teaspoon ground cumin
¼ teaspoon caraway seeds
chili powder, to taste
1 15-ounce can chickpeas
   (garbanzos)
2 spicy sausages (chorizo or
   longoniza), skinned, fried
   dry, and crumbled
salt, to taste
2 tablespoons minced parsley

San Angel, in the South of Mexico City, has a large German population. Some of these families have lived in Mexico for three generations, long enough to put a Teutonic stamp on some very delicious dishes.

There is a wonderful German delicatessen on Avenida Revolución in San Angel, which carries delicious, home-made veal sausages which can be substituted for the spicy ones in this recipe. I also confess to cheating on the garbanzo cooking—it's so easy to open a can, and the flavor difference is minimal in this zesty rendering.

1. Render the bacon, remove from the pan to paper towels, and add the vegetable oil to the bacon drippings. When the fats are hot, sauté the chopped onion, garlic, and tomatoes, adding the cumin, caraway seeds, and chili powder last. Let simmer for a few minutes.

2. Transfer to a large saucepan. Add the chickpeas with their own liquor, the sausage, and crumbled bacon. Season with salt to taste and cook until the mixture is thick.

3. Serve in heated bowls, sprinkled with parsley.

Note: This could be a main dish when served with a good rye bread and a crispy salad. Also, by adding three cups of good broth, you have a hearty winter soup.

CORONA DE FRIJOL

Crown of Beans

Serves 6

This recipe, a favorite of my children, came from an old Mexican cookbook and was "played with" by my inventive cook, Sabina. It makes a fine main course, or can be served as a side, with any meat dish. If you'd like a vegetarian version, omit the chorizo, and use a bit of vegetable oil instead of the chorizo fat.

2 cups pinto or red beans
6 cups water
4 tablespoons vegetable oil
1 clove garlic, peeled and mashed
6 ounces *Añejo* (Feta-type) cheese
2 chorizo sausages, chopped, and fried (see *Chorizo de Toluca* page 104)
1 medium-size onion, chopped
2 eggs, well beaten
½ teaspoon salt
½ cup bread crumbs

1. Cook the beans (see page 133). Drain.
2. Heat 2 tablespoons of vegetable oil in an iron skillet. Lightly brown the garlic. Add the beans, and continue cooking over me dium heat for about 10 minutes, mashing them with a fork. Add the cheese and mash together.
3. Fry the chorizo until crisp, crumbling it in the pan. Drain between pieces of paper towel, and sSet aside.
4. Add the onion, eggs, 1 tablespoon of vegetable oil from the chorizo, and salt to the bean mixture and mix well.
5. Grease a ring mold and sprinkle it with bread crumbs. Pour in the bean mixture and press it down well. Brush in the remaining oil and sprinkle with bread crumbs. Bake in a moderate oven (350°F) for about 15 minutes.
6. Remove the ring mold from the oven, invert it, sprinkle chorizo on top, and serve at once. You can fill the center of the mold with white rice or sprigs of watercress.

ENSALADA DE VERDURAS

Vegetable Salad

Serves 4

1 white turnip, cooked
2 carrots, cooked
2 large potatoes, peeled and
  boiled
1 small head cauliflower,
  cooked
2 tablespoons wine vinegar
3 tablespoons olive oil
½ teaspoon Dijon mustard
salt and pepper, to taste
½ cup peas, cooked
12 green stuffed olives,
  chopped
1 tablespoon capers
1 teaspoon parsley, minced fine

If ever a recipe deserved the adjective "ubiquitous," this is the one!

No torta, or simple entrée ever arrives at table without this mixed, cooked vegetable salad, usually drenched in mayonnaise and without flavor. I include it simply because it is everywhere in the cuisine. However, I've taken the liberty of using a spicy vinaigrette instead of mayonnaise, added a few "green things" for flavor and color, and undercooked the veggies "al dente."

1. Chop the turnip, carrots, potatoes, and cauliflower into small cubes.
2. Prepare a vinaigrette by whisking together the vinegar, olive oil, mustard, and salt and pepper.
3. Add the peas, chopped olives, capers, and parsley to the rest of the ingredients, and toss lightly with the vinaigrette. Refrigerate and allow the flavors to meld for several hours before serving.

PESCADO ENVINADO PICANTE

Bass with a Spicy Red Wine Sauce

Serves 6–8

½ teaspoon ground cumin
2 cloves of garlic
1 teaspoon Tabasco or other hot sauce
3 tablespoons vegetable oil
12 fish fillets
1 green pepper, chopped
3 tomatoes, peeled and chopped (canned may be substituted)
1 cup red wine
salt, to taste
½ teaspoon oregano
2 tablespoons fresh coriander/ cilantro, chopped
12 stuffed green olives
1 heaping tablespoon capers
olive oil

A special dispensation from Rome exempted the Mexican Catholic community from mandatory abstention from meat on Fridays. The reason is quite practical. The wisdom of the church was that in poor countries meat should be consumed when it is available, even on a Friday—and that abstaining one day a week, any day, will serve the good Lord well.

This recipe is inspired by a dish served in the famous Lincoln Restaurant in Mexico City. A snowy seabass was the star on the plate, but the recipe works well with any firm-fleshed fish.

1. Grind together the cumin and garlic, and moisten with the Tabasco to make a paste.
2. In a large, heavy-bottomed skillet, heat the vegetable oil and fry the fish lightly, removing when it starts to brown. In the remaining oil, sauté the green pepper. Add the garlic paste, and lastly, add the chopped tomatoes. Let simmer for 5 minutes. Add the red wine and simmer for another minute. Season with salt.
3. In a greased, ovenproof dish, place layers of fish, tomato and wine sauce, oregano, coriander, olives, and capers. Spoon the sauce over each layer and drizzle lightly with olive oil. Cover with aluminum foil and allow the flavor to develop for several hours in the refrigerator. Bring to room temperature before baking.
4. Preheat the oven to 350°F and bake the fish for 30–40 minutes, until heated through. Serve at once with rice or a simple potato dish, and of course, a glass of red wine.

LANGOSTINOS AL MOJO DE AJO

. . . .

Rock Lobsters¹ in Garlic

Serves 6

36 rock lobsters in their shells
    (you may substitute jumbo
    shrimp)
15 cloves garlic, 3 whole,
    12 minced
¾ teaspoon salt
¾ teaspoon freshly ground
    pepper
¾ teaspoon white vinegar
3 tablespoons olive oil
5 tablespoons butter
3 tablespoons lime juice

1. From the underside, split the shellfish down the middle without separating them completely from their shells. Remove the dark vein if apparent.
2. In a blender, purée the whole garlic cloves, salt, pepper, and vinegar. Marinate the shrimp in this mixture for 30 minutes.

Bellinghausen is a venerable "Once-German" restaurant in Mexico's famous "Pink Zone." The food is marvelous, and the service, a cross between brash and fawning—depending upon who you are and the waiter's disposition of the moment. Seated, enclosed in its charming patio filled with pots of flowers circling a tinkling fountain, you can imagine for a moment that the raucous and polluted city outside is at bay, conveniently halted for your mealtime pleasure.

One afternoon we had a double floorshow—a sudden, sharp earth tremor emptied all of the water in the fountain over the side in a huge wave, and into the shoes of the nearest patrons—a humorous counterpoint for the usual nervousness that a quake occasions. Mexicans truly adore slapstick!

(Continued)

3. In a large, heavy skillet, heat the oil and butter. Add the minced garlic and sauté until golden brown, about 3 minutes. Add the shellfish with the shell sides up. Lower the heat, cover, and cook for 2–3 minutes, or until the rock lobsters or shrimp are opaque.

4. Sprinkle with the lime juice and remove from the heat. Serve immediately, swimming in the garlic sauce, with good bread for sopping.

Just as everyone had settled down, including the unwilling "surfed" table occupants, a waiter, still apprehensive but carrying on in the best serving tradition, emerged from the kitchen carrying a gargantuan tray of dozens of these, Langostinos al Mojo de Ajo. *Turning to look at the fountain, his toe hit the step to the second level and the tray took off like an errant missile— showering 50 patrons with oil, garlic, and* langostinos. *I remember one balding gentleman pawing off two of the slippery critters which had lodged in one ear and under the last few of his prized hairs. The reaction was: gasps— applause— noisy indignation, and finally, helpless laughter. What a sight. I'll never enjoy this dish without a chuckle at the memory.*

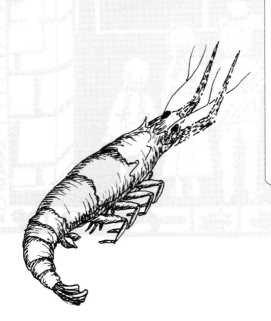

[1] Also called "spiny lobsters" or *langoustines* in French.

LENGUA DE RES ESTILO LA MERCED

Tongue, Market-style

Serves 4

3–4 pound fresh beef tongue
1/2 cup lemon juice
4 carrots, sliced
2 teaspoons thyme
1 teaspoon oregano
1 bay leaf
10 whole cloves
12 peppercorns, whole
1 large onion, sliced
1 clove garlic, minced

Sauce:
2 tablespoons vegetable oil
3 cloves garlic, minced
1 medium-sized onion, grated
3/4 cup orange juice
1/2 cup golden raisins
1 tablespoon orange zest
1 tablespoon cider vinegar
6 plum tomatoes, peeled and
    seeded (may use canned)
1/2–1 4-ounce can chopped
    Jalapeño peppers (depends
    on your taste)

The next time you have the opportunity to visit Mexico City, take a morning off and go to the new Merced Market.

The old Market has been razed . . . a fact which deserves praise, but also brings forth nostalgia. It was singular in its genre of immense, open markets; unique in that it was simultaneously the centre for both retail and wholesale food distribution for the world's largest city; and mind-boggling in its depth and variety of product selection. Everything from herbs to toys, kitchen utensils to fresh flowers, wild game, both caged and dressed, piece goods to edible barnacles, and separate buildings dedicated to the confectioners' art and straw artifacts.

The new market is more organized and a good deal cleaner, but I must admit, I liked the old one better! This recipe is an approximation of a fragrant order of beef tongue that I enjoyed many years ago at one of the Merced restoranes.

1. Wash the tongue well and let stand in water to cover mixed with the lemon juice. Let soak overnight. Drain.

2. Place the tongue in large pot with 4 quarts of fresh water, and the remaining ingredients. Cook very slowly until tender (4–6 hours or 45 minutes in a pressure cooker). Allow to cool in the liquid.

3. Prepare the sauce by heating the oil in a sauté pan and sautéing the garlic and onion for a few minutes until soft.

4. In a small saucepan, heat the orange juice, and allow the raisins to sit in the hot juice, covered, until they are plump. Add the orange zest, vinegar, tomatoes, and Jalapeño peppers and simmer for 3–4 minutes to meld the flavors. Set aside, keeping warm.

5. Peel off the rough skin of the tongue. Slice the tongue thin and serve with some sauce drizzled over the slices, and the remaining sauce on the side. Serve with tiny new potatoes browned in oil and garlic.

Note: This sweet and sour sauce is used with many offal meats, much like the gremolata and fruited mustard combination used in Italian cookery.

PASTEL DE MÓCTEZUMA

Aztec Pie

Serves 8

1 whole chicken,[1] stewed
12 tortillas
2 tablespoons vegetable oil
salt and pepper, to taste
2 cups *Salsa Verde* (page 169)
1 cup white cheese, grated or
   crumbled (mild Cheddar,
   Feta, or Parmesan)
1 cup crème fraîche or thinned
   sour cream

1. Shred the chicken meat (you should have about 3 cups) and set aside.
2. Cut the tortillas into 3/4-inch strips. In a medium-sized skillet, heat the oil and quick-fry the strips until slightly browned but still pliable.
3. Place half the tortillas in the bottom of an ovenproof casserole. Top with half of the chicken. Season with salt and pepper. Drizzle half the *Salsa Verde* on top. Sprinkle with half the cheese and spread with half the cream.
4. Repeat with the remaining ingredients. Cover with aluminum foil and bake for 20–25 minutes at 350°F, or until heated through. Remove the foil and continue baking for an additional 5–10 minutes until the top is lightly browned and bubbly.

The passion for a specific place often has to do with the people who inhabit it. Two beloved friends who made Mexico welcoming, exciting, and finally "home" are Max and Helen Grunstein. How many unforgettable hours we spent as intertwined families, drinking, laughing, and above all, eating.

Helen, along with her kitchen duendes (*elves*), served this special version of an ancient standard at many happy fiestas, my fortieth birthday party included. Whenever I prepare it for new friends, the background memory of mariachis, mirth, and the beautiful Casa Grunstein is with me always. Please serve it with love—it's an essential ingredient.

---

[1] Pie may also be made using shredded pork.

POLLOS EN ZANAORIA

Chicken in Carrot Sauce

I've included this recipe for historical value—please do not try to correct and prepare. Note the "stream of consciousness" cook's notes. The book was hand-written before the Mexican Revolution. More about its origins is unknown, but it has its unpunctuated charm. Courtesy of Ing. Gregorio Lifshitz, President of Productos Metálicos Standard, S.A., Mexico City.

This is a translation of a recipe from the "Libro de Cocina de los beneficios de cada cosa, y sus compuestos" (Kitchen book) outlining the benefits of each thing and its ingredients."

"Make a broth with chopped onion, a half a handful of chopped tomatillos, two cloves of garlic chopped tomatoes some green chiles refried in lard with a bit of water when the latter is fried add a little water, and a little more in which you cooked the chicken, and measure three cloves of garlic, mashed and chopped carrots, chick peas cooked with *[tequesquite?]*[1] cook until it boils and add parsley, little pieces of cooked ham, $\frac{1}{2}$ cup of vinegar, lots of saffron, cumin, pepper, whole cloves, bread crumbs, capers, olives, chilies and parsley."

---

[1] Náhuatl word whose precise translation has been lost.

CARNE ASADA A LA TAMPIQUEÑA

Flank Steak, Tampico-style

Serves 4

Carne Asada is less a recipe than a blueprint, or, at the very least, a simple listing of ingredients, the recipes for which are to be found elsewhere in these pages. Attributing the recipe to the gulfport of Tampico is colorful, but not accurate. Actually, the dish was first "constructed," and subsequently popularized, by a famous restaurateur from Tampico, José Inés Loredo.

4 skirt steaks, no thicker than
   ¼-inch
salt and pepper, to taste
Refried Beans (see page 28)
Mexican White Rice
   (see page 132)
Poblano peppers, sautéed
   (Rajas, see page 433)
Guacamole, omitting the
   bacon (see page 25)
8 tortillas
Salsa Verde (see page 169)
Feta cheese, crumbled
onion slices for garnish

1. Lightly salt and pepper the steaks and quick grill or pan fry to the dsired doneness; rare, medium, or well done.

2. On an oval heated dish, arrange a portion each of Refried Beans, white rice, sautéed peppers, and Guacamole.

3. Lightly coat each tortilla with oil (I use a spray), and warm in a sauté pan just long enough to absorb the oil and soften. Remove from the pan and spread each tortilla with *Salsa Verde*, folding over in half. Place at one end of the serving dish, and garnish with Feta cheese and onion slices.

PEPITOS EL COYOTE

Filled Ground Meat Patties

Serves 4

This wonderful variation on the hamburger theme was a menu favorite at the small Coyoacán Restaurant, El Coyote Flaco, and at home with my hungry brood. It was served with the ubiquitous white rice and delicious beans "drunken-style" (see page 47).

1½ pounds lean chopped sirloin
2 teaspoons Worcestershire sauce (called *Salsa Inglesa* in Mexico)
1 clove garlic, mashed
1 egg yolk
1 cup finely chopped boiled ham
½ cup shredded, white Cheddar cheese
⅓ cup raisins, plumped
⅓ cup chopped green pepper
2–3 tablespoons vegetable oil

1. Mix the sirloin, Worcestershire, garlic, and egg yolk well; divide into 4 portions. On wax paper, roll the meat into circles 9 to 10 inches across.

2. Just to the center of each meat circle lay equal amounts of ham, cheese, raisins, and green pepper. Fold half of the circle over, forming a half moon. Pinch the edges together slightly.

3. Heat the oil in a large skillet and fry the half moons on one side until brown. Flip and cook the other side until the meat is cooked and the filling is warm and runny (about 3 minutes). Serve at once with *Salsa Mexicana* (page 168) on the side.

FILETE SICILIANO LA GONDOLA

Spiced Skirt Steak

Serves 4

3 tablespoons extra virgin
  olive oil
4 cloves garlic, peeled and
  mashed
8 whole cloves
drizzle of balsamic vinegar
4 beef skirt steaks
salt and pepper, to taste

La Góndola is a wonderful, small restaurant in Mexico City's Zona Rosa (Pink Zone). The restaurant was started by a gifted young Italian immigrant chef, whose culinary fame became such that he "cooked" himself a title, a Dukedom, I believe. This simple recipe is my own recreation of a dish we enjoyed at least once a week on Genova Street. You may also want to try his Spaghetti Carbonara— it's the best I've ever eaten.

1. In a heavy, iron skillet the heat the olive oil and sauté the garlic and whole cloves for 1½ minutes. Empty the pan and reserve 2 tablespoons of the oil and the garlic. Discard the cloves.
2. Quick pan fry the steaks in oil to the desired doneness, and turn out onto heated platter.
3. Deglaze the pan with balsamic vinegar and the reserved garlic and oil. Pour over the steaks. Salt and pepper, and serve at once.

OSTIONES EN GUISADO DE CHIPOTLE

. . . .

Smoked Chile Oyster Stew

Serves 4

3 dozen fresh oysters in the
    shell
2 tablespoons cooking oil
1 large onion, grated
2 garlic cloves, peeled and
    bruised
6 ripe tomatoes, peeled and
    chopped fine
4–6 canned chipotle chilies,
    rinsed, seeded, and deveined
2 cups oyster juice (may be extended with clam juice)
1 shot glass white tequila (vodka may be substituted)
juice of half a fresh lime
salt, to taste
fresh lime slices

I first tasted this robust dish in the home of friends in Mexico City. It's one of those dishes which tickles your nose before it stuns your palate. This "stew" is meant to be eaten by dipping into the mass with a chunk of bolillo (French-type hard roll) and capturing an oyster. It doesn't make for elegant eating . . . but oh, is it memorable! Of course, serve it with a a mug of a favorite Mexican beer, or pair it with more tequila in a frosty margarita.

1. Shuck the oysters, carefully straining and reserving the juice. Put into a cool place until serving time.
2. In a large, heavy skillet, heat the oil and sauté the onion and garlic until transparent.
3. Drop the tomatoes into boiling water for 2 minutes. Pierce the skins, peel, and chop.
4. In a large saucepan, combine the chopped tomatoes with the chipotle chilies and oyster juice, and simmer a few minutes to allow the flavors to meld.
5. Add the tequila and lime juice. Allow the mixture to cook down until it is the consistency of thick gravy. Add salt to taste.
6. Divide the oysters into 4 to 6 individual earthenware casseroles. Have the sauce piping hot and pour over the oysters. Garnish with lime slices, and serve accompanied by bite-sized chunks of crispy-crusted, French-type bread.

CARNITAS LOS PANCHOS

Tacos of Twice-Cooked Pork

Serves 4

2 pounds pork leg
3 garlic cloves, peeled and
   mashed
1 large onion, halved
2 large carrots, peeled
4 whole cloves
2 bay leaves
1 teaspoon oregano
1/2 teaspoon cumin
chicken or beef broth
salt and pepper, to taste

Long after you've left the country you've lived in for many years, you find yourself dreaming about it, and often, in the language of the land. My most frequent dreams in Spanish are about a small taquería called Los Panchos, near Chapultepec Park, in Mexico City. The tacos are divine—warm, fragrant, and wrapped in brown butcher paper. They are most often consumed standing in front of the counter, watching the cooks energetically wield their cleavers— and the aroma of the spiced pork will be with me always! Me da dos por favor, con chicharrón y chiquita![1]

1. Cut the meat into 1-inch cubes, leaving any fat on.
2. Place in a large pot with the remaining ingredients (except the salt and pepper) and enough broth to cover. Bring to a boil, lower the heat, and allow to simmer for 2 hours. Check from time to time, and add more broth if needed.
3. Drain the meat. (Strain the broth and store as a soup or sauce base.)
4. Place the meat cubes in an extended, oven-proof pan and add salt and pepper to taste. Bake for 45–50 minutes at 350°F, turning the meat once.
5. Remove from the oven and shred the meat with two forks while still warm. Place in the center of a hot tortilla and serve with your favorite chili sauce, chopped onions, and chopped coriander/cilantro.

---

[1] "Give me two please, with cracklings and rendered fat!"

NARANJAS BORRACHAS

Frozen Drunken Oranges

Yield: 16 servings[1]

Sabina, my jewel of a cook, would spend hours over a hot stove preparing the mid-day comida, *but when it came to desserts, "quick and easy" were her by-words. Because fruits are one of Mexico's glories, here is one of her simple specialties.*

8 ripe juice oranges,
    unblemished
½ cup mashed strawberries
    (may use frozen)
1 pint orange sherbet, softened
2 tablespoons tequila
2 tablespoons orange liqueur
2 tablespoons lime or lemon juice
sugar, to taste
mint sprigs, for garnish

1. Cut the oranges in half crosswise and, handling like a grapefruit half, section out the pulp. Place in a medium-sized mixing bowl.
2. Remove the membrane from the empty skin halves, scraping away as much of the pith as possible without breaking through the skin.
3. Chop and mix the orange pieces with the strawberries, sherbet, tequila, liqueur, and juice. Add sugar if it's too sour for your taste.
4. Spoon the mixture back into the orange shells and freeze for several hours until solid. Serve each half on crushed ice in sherbet cups or bowls, garnished with a sprig of mint.

---

[1] This recipe makes a double batch because the filled oranges freeze so well. I also imagine that Sabina made double so that her ubiquitous visiting family might also enjoy the sweet!

AMERENGADO DE CHOCOLATE

Chocolate Fluff Dessert

Serves 6

1 small package cream cheese
1 tablespoon milk
1 teaspoon vanilla
2½ cups confectioners' sugar, well sifted
dash of salt
1 8-ounce bar of unsweetened chocolate, melted
1 cup heavy cream, whipped stiff
½ cup nuts (hazelnuts or pistachios)

Because Mexico City is so cosmopolitan, you will find many recipes which seem familiar to all ethnic backgrounds. This one is a combination of French and Italian influences, with the very North American use of cream cheese. I have not tried to make this a healthy dessert, simply a delicious one, so serve it in judicious amounts—just a dollop to sweeten an after dinner palate.

1. In a large bowl, blend the cheese with the milk and vanilla until you have a smooth paste.
2. Add the sugar, little by little, until it is all incorporated. Add the salt, and blend in the melted chocolate.
3. Fold in the heavy cream until you have a heavy froth. Divide equally into individual cups, and top with chopped nuts of your choice.

BUDÍN DE LIMÓN

Lemon Pudding

Serves 4

2 tablespoons of all-purpose
   flour
½–⅔ cup sugar
pinch of salt
1 tablespoon butter, melted
3 tablespoons lemon juice
zest of the lemon
2 eggs, yolks separated from
   whites
⅔ cup milk

Sanborn's House of Tile in Mexico City is not only a historical landmark, but it serves some of the best regional Mexican cuisine in the Capital. I remember sitting in the noisy indoor patio, people watching, when the waitperson, dressed in her starched adaptation of an indigenous costume, trilled something about the "dessert special of the day." That dessert became one of my favorite recipes, and here it is for your pleasure.

1. Blend together the flour, sugar, and salt. Add the butter making a smooth paste.
2. Blend the lemon juice and zest with the beaten egg yolks and the milk. Set aside.
3. Beat the egg whites until they form peaks, and fold into the lemon mixture.
4. Pour into individual custard cups, and place the cups in a shallow baking pan with the water level to 1-inch up the cups. Bake in a 300°F oven until a knife inserted along side of custard comes away clean, about 30 minutes. Cool on a rack.

CHISME

A MEXICAN COLONIAL BAR MITZVAH

Until you've heard "Hava Nageela" played by a hot mariachi band, you haven't lived!

Mexicans are enormously creative, and you can't live in their country for as long as we did, without absorbing some of their constant quest for new art forms.

When our older son, Carl, approached the important age of Jewish manhood, and was slaying his own intellectual demons of yet another language to learn (and one written backwards!), I began to obsess about having a Bar Mitzvah celebration that was "different!"

I will say here, that "one-upsmanship" is not confined to the Anglo culture. Unless your youngster is the oldest in his class, by the time it becomes your jewel's turn to approach the Torah, you've already been a guest at several of these post-Temple extravaganzas . . . and your maternal wheels are spinning, no matter what your ethnicity.

Number one son intoned: "We need dance music Mom," then slyly, ". . . could we have it at the San Angel Inn . . . and lots of food, but really good food, and . . ."

Let me pause here to relate that my children did not consider anything approaching "fast" food—*good* food—no way!

Because they had been taken from the breast to adult gourmet fare puréed in the blender—good food, meant epicurean stuff, great variety, exotically seasoned, and *expensive!*

The San Angel Inn was a favorite dining spot for the whole family–a former Hacienda, nunnery, and then art school, restored magnificently, with superb service, and marvelous food. But you think that a Mexican Colonial treasure seemed an odd place for a Jewish post-religious celebration, well, what the hey!—we did it, and it was grand!!!!

Cocktails and soft drinks for the young teenagers were served in the formal gardens to the rear. Hors d'oeuvres included: tiny tacos with a fiery guacamole dip, fried tortilla chips rolled in chili powder and confectioners' sugar; *garnachas* filled with chorizo and potato blends; and *sopes* filled with—ready for this—chopped liver! (The Inn chef jazzed up my recipe with a bit of brandy . . . not bad. I make it that way to this day!)

The main course was chicken, with a choice of *mole* or Gringo pan gravy for the less adventuresome. There was white rice and some sort of wonderful salad, and the Inn's signature vanilla Bavaroise dusted with cinnamon, sharing honors with the Bar Mitzvah boy's monumental cake.

Here's where the emphasis left Jerusalem and headed for Jalisco! The cake was brought in by two impeccably-clad waiters (their uniform is a variation of the Charro outfits, silver-trimmed black trousers, snowy shirts, and multihued, fringed, silk string ties) and they were preceded and accompanied by the sweetest Mariachi trumpet you've ever heard, playing the "Diana." The Diana is a musical tribute played at the bullrings when something splendid happens, a particularly nice move by either the bull or the *torero*.

Well, in Mexican terms, several years of Hebrew study, perfectly completed and demonstrated, rated a Diana . . . my handsome son blushed furiously and everyone gasped, then applauded wildly.

The Mariachis played all afternoon into the evening. The kids, twisted, frugged, and bamba'd, and finally, as a salute to the grandparents present, and the less agile guests, The Mariachi Menendez swung into the hottest "hora" you ever heard! . . . A Mexican mazel tov! . . . Ole!

EL BAJÍO

States of

SAN LUIS POTOSÍ, MICHOACÁN, GUANAJUATO, QUERÉTARO, AQUASCALIENTES

EL BAJIO

Bajío translates to the "low place," correctly christened only in comparison to the soaring, rugged Sierras which surround this vast, lush plateau. The villages and towns of this region house some of Mexico's greatest treasures in crops, crafts, and cuisine.

Heavy Spanish colonial influence is to be found in the baroque architecture and interiors of the churches and cathedrals of the cities of Morelia, Guanajuato, San Miguel Allende, and Dolores Hidalgo.

More Iberian brushstrokes which color the brilliant canvas of the Bajío are the stone aqueducts undulating across rolling landscape; the concentric plodding of oxen as they turn the giant mill wheels of the *norias* (water wheels), which are used to grind corn; and the bray of *burritos*—the noble, small beasts of burden brought originally from Europe to lighten the loads of the new continent.

Each city or town, regardless of its size, prides itself on a particular festival, craft, or delicacy, or a combination of all. The local and varying cuisine of the Bajío dramatically reflects its European roots, mixed with the vigor and imagination of the Otomís, Tarascans,[1] and several smaller indigenous cultures.

The Mexican Indians' ingenious use of the lands' yield is defined in the multiple uses to which two particular cacti, omnipresent in the region, are put. Maguey leaves are used for everything from wrappers for singular, Mexican "en papilotte" delicacies to thread; shredded from dried spears and used to weave baskets and mats; or simply to sew sturdy, carrying and storage sacks.

Brilliant green stands of *nopales* (we know them as "prickly pear cactus"), act as boundary delineators and fences, as well as being prepared and enjoyed in a variety of ways on Mexican tables.

Nowhere in the Bajío must you go hungry—there is too much natural bounty coaxed by the peerless creativity of its cooks to tempt the adventuresome diner.

---

[1] The prideful Purépechas to save face, called the Spaniards who had pillaged and raped their daughters, *tarascue*, "son-in-law." The name was later bastardized to *Tarascan*, the name commonly used now. The old name appears in many places today. The first-class express train from Mexico City is called "The Purépecha."

THINGS TO SEE, DO, AND EAT

San Juan del Río: From the Capital, a sort of gateway to the Bajío, this is a good shopping town for semiprecious stones (opals) from nearby Trinidad mines, in particular.

Tequisquiapan: Check on the annual wine and cheese festival (May); the fanciful wicker work in the shape of baskets, animals, mats, and more, and the vineyards producing creditable wine.

Querétaro: This is the home of the second level of de-centralized government. In its environs, lovely old haciendas are converted into stylish hotels, roadside cheese shops to try/buy local *patagrás*, manchego, and "Walter," a Swiss cheese-type.

Irapuato: The home of luscious, magenta strawberries sold by the side of the road from tall cylindrical baskets.

San Miguel de Allende: An artists' colony and retirement center for European and North American expatriates is located here. It is also a veritable treasure trove of decorator items, crafts, and fine art.

Guanajuato: The colonial gem of the Bajío offers serpentine, stone-cobbled streets so narrow that local lovers will often share kisses from balconies on opposite sides of the passage. It is famous for mummies and other ghoulish mementos—and with the wry humor of the Mexicans, sugar replicas of those mummies, hawked in front of every public place. And the annual,\ month-long Cervantes Festival is a multilingual glut for the intellect.

Dolores Hidalgo: Note here the beautiful Spanish-style glazed tile work and historic memorabilia of Father Hidalgo, the father of Mexican independence from Spain.

San Luis Potosí: This is the home for a dozen roseate-façaded churches decorated, both inside and out, with fanciful carvings (do not miss the buildings abutting the Jardín Hidalgo plaza), rustic wood marquetry prized in antique markets worldwise, the Good Friday religious processions, and silk rebozos so fine they can be pulled through a bride's wedding ring.

Aguascalientes: The center of breeding ranches for the fighting bulls of the Fiesta Brava is found here. The annual San Marcos agricultural fair (April) is for all lovers of the bullfight, where the animals are viewed and "tried" *(la tienta)* for the bravery of their blood and bloodlines.

> *Note:* Going due west from Mexico City to approach the Bajío from another angle, you will head through the unattractive town of H.

Zitácuaro, (the "H" is an honorary designation for "heroic," referring to Zitácuaro's brilliant showing in a battle during Pancho Villa's
time). Ignore the trucks, you are en route to my favorite area, glorious Michoacán.

San José Purúa: A detour worth the few miles from Zitácuaro. One of Mexico's
most beautiful spas, with spectacular gorge views and several kinds of spa waters;
hot, cool, sulphury, bubbly, sensuous, and wonderful.

Morelia: Someone called it a "very Spanish city in a very indigenous area"—
this fascinating state capital is the marketing center for the myriad crafts which
spring from the talented fingers of the Indians of the area. The downtown
craftsmarket, next to the Cathedral, is a "must see." Up the hill, in the town of
Santa María de Güido, is one of Mexico's most famous inns, The Villa Montana,
and a furniture and fine woodworking shop, "El Señal."

Pátzcuaro: This is the home of the famed *Día de los Muertos* (Day of the
Dead) celebration. Butterfly net fishermen, transparent, but deliciously edible
white fish from the lake, and more wonderful crafts can be found.

Paracho: Here we have a cottage industry with a village attached—lovingly
crafted guitars prized worldwide.

Uruapan: This city is noted for extraordinary lacquer work, where the many
layers of color are painstakingly burnished, and then the intricate designs incised
in the built-up lacquer surface.

Apatzingán: The melon capital of the world.

CHISME

URUAPAN

Mud and Memories

As the original optimist, I am always irrevocably convinced that wherever I go, I will find an undiscovered little jewel of a restaurant.

Surprisingly, this positive or optimistic attitude often works. I remember an experience years ago in a small, muddy Mexican town called Uruapan. It was the "raining season" as my daughter calls it and the cobbled streets ran with sepia-colored sludge. After half an hour of cussing and sliding around, we noticed a doe-eyed youngster waving at us. She was miming the gesture common to the country—four fingers held tightly together and jabbed towards the mouth. It means, ". . . are you hungry, well, let's eat!!"

The sign language was implicit enough to put salivary glands "on the ready." We nodded enthusiastically, and skated along after her for a block or two. A mammoth, termite-ventilated door opened to her special knock and, oh my—after a tentative tip-toeing down a long, dark, dirt-floored entry—we emerged into a toile-hung, country French drawing room—in Uruapan!

A blazing fireplace welcomed us with a view to a rushing, vine over-hung stream. Four tables were set with fine linen, Wedgewood china, and sparkling baccarat. Brahms swirled around us and we were greeted by a red-bearded giant who thanked the child with a coin.

That evening's meal was exquisite—the location was 120 percent *pueblito* (village), but the repast, service, and conversation were total "sophisticated Capitals of the world."

Our host/chef introduced himself as Count Someone (an expatriate French nobleman?!). The Count, a declared runaway from civilization (to write a family history as I remember, although it's not germane to the anecdote), treated us as honored guests. The men traded war stories (they had both flown in WWII and known aeronautical genius, Fokker), tinkered over a hi-fi system with the megrims, and ended the evening pleasantly tipsy and friends.

So much for being adventurous—with tempered caution, a growling belly and a smile in both your heart and on your lips, the most delightful dining experiences may await you.

MINGUICHI

Cheese Soup, Tarascan-style

Serves 6

Called by the Tarascan word in the State of Michoacán, this soup is also made in Oaxaca. The variations have largely to do with the cheeses made in each region.

Imagine a steaming bowl of Minguichi, served in the fancifully-painted green and brown pottery bowls from Tzintzuntzán, while enjoying the ballet of the nets of the Lake Pátzcuaro fishermen.

4 Poblano chilies (see page 43)
6 medium-sized tomatoes, peeled and quartered
1 tablespoon vegetable oil
2 teaspoons butter or margarine
1 medium-sized onion, grated or chopped fine
1 clove garlic, minced
4 medium-sized potatoes, cut in small cubes
2 cups corn kernels
5 cups chicken broth
2 cups milk
salt and pepper, to taste
½ pound *queso manchego* (or Romano), diced
1 small mozzarella cheese, diced.

1. Prepare Poblano chilies (see page 43) or substitute canned chipotles, rinsing and seeding the chilies, then slicing them into fine strips (julienne).
2. In a blender, purée the tomatoes, strain, and set aside.
3. Heat the oil and butter together in a skillet, add the onion, garlic, potatoes, and corn, and sauté for 5 minutes.
4. Add the puréed tomatoes and simmer, uncovered, for 5 minutes. Stir in the broth and simmer for 10 minutes or until potatoes are tender. Add the chile strips and cook for 5 minutes. Add the milk and simmer for 5 more minutes. Taste and season with salt and pepper.
5. Before serving, divide the cheeses among 6 soup bowls. Pour the hot soup over, stir, and serve with heated French-type rolls (*bollilos*).

SOPA DE AJO Y TOMILLO

Garlic and Thyme Soup

Serves 4

This soup must have crept into the Mexican recipe repertoire on little Spanish feet— whatever, it's often found on fine city menus all over Mexico. This is my own recipe which evolved from a steaming version I once enjoyed in Guanajuato.

Warning: Don't be spooked by the amount of garlic—the cooking tames it nicely.

½ cup olive oil
2 medium-sized heads garlic, broken into cloves and unpeeled
1 cup (scant) stale bread cubes
1 quart beef stock
2 teaspoons sweet pimiento, chopped
1 small sprig fresh thyme
salt and pepper, to taste
2 eggs, beaten (or 4 whole eggs[1])

1. In a medium-sized, heavy skillet, heat the oil and sauté the *unpeeled* garlic until slightly golden. Now, slip off and discard the garlic skins, returning "nude" cloves to the skillet.
2. While the stock is heating separately in a 2- to 3-quart pot, sauté the bread cubes in the oil and garlic mixture until the bread becomes slightly brown.
3. Once the stock reaches boiling point, add the bread, garlic and olive oil, chopped sweet pimiento, and the sprig of thyme. Allow to boil for 3 minutes, remove the thyme sprig, and purée the mixture in a blender or food processor. Before serving, stir in beaten eggs, adjust the seasoning, and garnish with the thyme sprig.

---

[1] Another popular version brings the puréed broth to a rolling boil before serving in individual heated bowls. One raw egg per person is then dropped into the bowls to quick poach and served immediately.

MOLE,
A CRAZY
MIXED-UP
DISH

(Pronounced moh´-lay, please)

Mole, which comes from the Spanish verb *moler*: to grind, and/or the Náhuatl (Aztec) word *molli*, which means a "mixture," is commonly underestimated as "that chocolate sauce." Scurrilous indeed, if you consider that a small square of bitter chocolate is only one of some 20 ingredients, painstakingly blended to confound even the most gifted food detective.

The best known of the many moles, *Mole Poblano*, comes to us from the colonial city of Puebla. A few of the exotic contents of this ambrosial sauce are three different kinds of toasted chili peppers, coriander, sesame and anise seeds, and almonds (see page 96, for the recipe).

Who invented *Mole Poblano* (Turkey in Mole Sauce)? The most repeated legend concerns Sor Andrea, the Mother Superior of the Convento de Santa Rosa. She is said to have concocted the dish to honor the Archbishop's visit, and to illustrate how well European traditions melded with those of the New World. The seasonings were a symbolic blend of both cultures.

My favorite account tells of an eager, young friar who was caught with an empty larder (no uncommon occurrence), when the illustrious Don Juan de Palafox y Mendoza paid an unannounced visit. The panicked friar scurried around, and with prayers and ingenuity, coaxed all the kitchen leftovers into a huge, earthenwear *cazuela*. A sympathetic parishioner's gift turkey became the base for the historic dinner.

Although outside of Mexico the *Mole Poblano* is the best known of the savory mixtures, each region of Mexico has its own version. Oaxaca is home of *Mole Amarillo* (Yellow Mole), whose color originates from a squash flower base, and a local, golden chili pepper. The central plateau is the Motherland of *Mole Verde* (Green Mole), a sister sauce which owes its verdancy to fresh coriander, green tomatillos, and ground pumpkin seeds. The sauce, also called *Pipián Verde de Pepita* (see page 240), is an absolute party fare at my house . . . an exciting accompaniment for pork or poultry—I've even served it with lamb. It is the one dish my far-flung family requests whenever we have our infrequent, but nonetheless, joyous and food-filled reunions.

Working through a recipe for any of the *moles*, it is easy to see why Mexican haute cuisine has taken so long to cross the Rio Grande. In our time restricted society, the hours of preparation necessary for a culinary "tour-de-force" like *mole*, preclude it from most ordinary menus. Imagination, dedication, and **love** are three *mole* ingredients **not** to be found in the ethnic food stores.

One other brief comment; there are two world famous **great** sauces—Indian curry and *Mole Poblano*. They both irrevocably . . . you, your party clothes, the upholstery, and the carpet. Please beware, and use disposable place mats and large, large, paper napkins!

SOPA MICHOACANA

Sweet Corn Soup

Serves 6

12 ears of sweet corn
3 cups milk, scalded
2 tablespoons butter
1 medium-sized onion, chopped
    fine
1 large tomato, peeled and chopped
½ teaspoon salt
⅛ teaspoon pepper
1 3-ounce package cream cheese, chunked
chili powder

> *Most corn in Mexico has fat, irregular kernels, and a tendency to be tough. Michoacán is one of the areas where a small kerneled, sugary variety is treasured. This is one of the few recipes where oil cannot be substituted for butter . . . the taste changes drastically.*

1. Cut the kernels from the cob and divide it into 2 portions. Mix 1 portion with the milk. Purée in the blender and set aside.

2. In a medium-sized skillet, melt the butter and sauté the remaining corn with the onion. Blend in the tomato, salt, pepper, and cream cheese. Allow the flavors to meld over very low heat for about 5 minutes. Add to the corn and milk mixture.

3. Serve hot, garnished with a sprinkling of chili powder.

CHAYOTE RELLENO

Stuffed Chayote Squash

Serves 6

3 large chayotes (look for the
　ones without spines, they
　handle easier)
2 tablespoons vegetable or light
　olive oil
3 cloves garlic, peeled and
　minced
1 small onion, grated
6 tablespoons seasoned bread
　crumbs
1 teaspoon chopped parsley
½ cup milk
½ teaspoon oregano
salt and pepper, to taste
4 tablespoons crumbled white
　cheese (like Feta or Parmesan

Chayote squash is pale green, sometimes spiny, pear-shaped, and quite delicious. Don't let unfamiliarity spook you. Because its flavor is so delicate, it lends itself to a spectrum of culinary experimentation. Steamed and chopped, it makes a fine salad when tossed with a garlicky vinaigrette, some chopped onion, and cilantro (see page 111). In Veracruz they add tomato, Jalapeño chili, and green olives to the filling.

This version is a favorite, remembered from a delicious Sunday brunch at the Hacienda Jurica outside of Querétaro on the road to San Luís Potosí.

1. Cut the chayotes in half and cook in water to cover until tender when pierced with a fork, about 30 minutes. Do not overcook or they will not hold their shape for stuffing. Cool.
2. In a skillet, heat the oil and sauté the garlic and onion until transparent.
3. Scoop out the chayote flesh with a spoon, taking care not to tear the tough outside. Set the shells aside. In a medium-sized mixing bowl, mix the cooked chayote, garlic and onion, bread crumbs, parsley, milk, and oregano. Blend well and add salt and pepper to taste.
4. Mound the filling in the shells and top with grated cheese. Bake at 350°F for 20–30 minutes until the filling is heated through.

Note: This stuffing works for almost any mild-flavored squash.

SALSA MEXICANA
(PICO DE GALLO)

No translation needed—this is the classic, fresh sauce, made daily (it ferments if not consumed the same day), which graces every table in the country. Its simple crunch and dashing mixture of flavors heightens any dish.

Yield: About 1½ cups sauce

> 5 serrano chilies (more or less, depending on your tolerance for spice)
> 3 large tomatoes
> 1 good-sized white onion
> a handful of fresh coriander/cilantro leaves
> 3 tablespoons olive oil
> salt and pepper, to taste

1. Heat a skillet and *torear*[1] the chilies, removing them before they burn or the skin breaks.
2. Working with gloves, halve the chilies lengthwise, remove the seeds and veins, and chop fine.
3. Chop the rest of the ingredients and blend with the olive oil, and salt and pepper. Place in a pottery or glass dish.

[1] Bull fighters (*toreros*) "work" the bull before beginning the earnest business of dispatching him. They move him back and forth and across the ring with their capes to see which way he hooks. In Mexican culinary terms to "torear" chilies, means to move them back and forth in the pan so they heat evenly.

SALSA VERDE

. . . .

Green Sauce

Yield: Approximately 4 cups

> This is the second of the basic sauces in Mexican cuisine. This is delicious with pork, poultry, fish, or just spooned over a warm tortilla. Because it is cooked, it has a refrigerator life of several days. It can also be made in larger batches and frozen.

15 *tomatillos* husked or
   1 26-ounce can
5 chilies serranos, or
   3 Jalapeños
1 large onion, chopped
2 cloves garlic, peeled
large handful of coriander/cilantro, chopped
2 tablespoons vegetable oil
2 cups broth (chicken, beef, or vegetable)
salt and pepper, to taste

1. In a large saucepan, boil the tomatillos, chilies, onion, and 1 clove of garlic together for about 10 minutes. Place the mixture in a blender or food processor. (Set the saucepan aside. Do not wash.)
2. Add the fresh coriander/cilantro and the second clove of garlic to the mixture, and process until smooth but uniformly grainy.
3. In a large skillet, heat the oil (to the sizzle point when a drop of water is added), and sauté the mixture, stirring constantly, until it begins to turn several shades darker and thickens.
4. Return the cooked mixture to the first saucepan, add the broth, and bring to a boil. Lower the heat, and simmer until it reaches a medium sauce consistency. Taste and season with salt and pepper.

HUEVOS POTOSINOS

Egg Casserole, San Luís Potosí

Serves 6

1 pound of cooked spinach,
  chopped (frozen can be
  substituted)
3 tablespoons butter or
  margarine
1 tablespoon heavy cream
½ teaspoon nutmeg
salt and pepper, to taste
2 turns of the pepper mill
  (black peppercorns)
8 hard-cooked eggs, sliced
1¼ cups basic white sauce
1 tablespoon prepared hot
  mustard
½ cup grated, white Cheddar-like sharp cheese
6 *tortillas de harina* (the white, flour tortillas)

Real de Catorce (The Royal 14), was the name of a famous gold mine after which the now, almost ghost town, is named. The Real Hotel is an enchanting find, more an Inn than a commercial hostelry. Make sure you try their whole grain bread and some of their Italian specialties.

Eggs are an important part of the Mexican diet, and the provinces can turn out more palate-pleasing ways to serve them than any other culture. This simple green and golden dish is an example.

1. Grease a 2- or 3-quart, ovenware casserole. Heat the oven to 325°F.
2. Blend into the hot, cooked spinach, the butter, cream, nutmeg, salt, and pepper. Spoon into the casserole, smoothing out with a spatula.
3. Gently lay the hard-cooked eggs over the spinach bed. Blend the mustard into white sauce and pour over the eggs. Top with the grated cheese.
4. Bake for 12–15 minutes and serve immediately, spooned over hot tortillas.[1]

---

[1] An Anglicized version would be to serve it over toasted English muffins.

ENSALADA DE CORPUS CHRISTI

. . . .

Corpus Christi Salad

Serves 6–8

Dressing:
½ cup light olive oil
¼ cup lemon juice
salt, to taste (optional)

2 cups tender corn kernels
2 cups zucchini squash, cut
   into ¾-inch dice
1 cup young peas
1 large cucumber, peeled and
   cut into ¾-inch dice
3 firm pears, peeled and
   chunked
6 ripe, but firm, apricots,
   quartered length-wise
1 cup cherries or blueberries,
   pitted (see note)
2–3 ripe avocados, peeled, chunked, and tossed in lemon juice

1. Prepare the dressing by whisking together the olive oil, lemon juice,a nd salt.
2. Place all the fruits and vegetables on a large, deep-sided platter. Toss the vegetables and fruits lightly with the dressing and serve chilled.

Note: The original recipe calls for "capulín" berries which are not available, but are considered by many to be toxic. They're not— I've eaten them many times.

Mexican economist/historian Jose N. Iturriaga is the author of a scholarly treatise on tacos, tamales, and tortas, the mainstays of the Mexican diet. In the opening pages of his study he laments the loss of many venerable recipes—dishes that were ritually prepared for feast days. He shares this one, handed down from his maternal grandmother from Celaya, in the hopes that it will not be lost in the vagrant files of oral history.

In the Iturriaga household this salad was always served with lightly breaded veal cutlets.

GORDITAS DEL BAJÍO

....

Shrimp and Cactus Fritters

Serves 6

> The Bajío is cactus country. If you live in the American West, you probably have a green nopal cactus in your backyard, but for Easterners, many fine grocers have them ready for use in small cans. They have dozens of savory uses, and can be used interchangeably with string beans in salads or like dishes. Look elsewhere in these pages for how to deal with fresh cactus (very carefully)!

1 pound cooked shrimp
3 large potatoes, boiled and peeled
½ cup corn meal
½ cup (or one small can) cooked nopal cactus leaves, chopped
1 large egg, well beaten.
¼ cup all-purpose flour
½ cup vegetable shortening

1. Coarsely chop and blend together the shrimp, potatoes, corn meal, and cactus leaves.
2. Stir in the beaten egg and let the mixture rest for about 15 minutes.
3. Moisten your hands with cold water and form the mixture into patties. Dust with flour and fry until golden in hot shortening. Remove to paper towels to drain and place in a warm oven until ready to serve.

Note: These are delicious when served with a creamy guacamole (see page 25).

POLLO DE LUJO A LA COTÉ

. . . .

Chicken Villa Montaña

Serves 4

¼ cup vegetable oil
1 young chicken (3–4 pounds)
salt and pepper, to taste
1 cup stock
1 stick cinnamon
1 cup dry white wine
1 small glass Curaçao liqueur
¼ teaspoon Maggi or Kitchen
   Bouquet
juice of 1 lemon
1 tablespoon cornstarch
1 tablespoon of cold water
2 oranges, peeled and sliced
½ pound Malaga grapes,
   peeled and seeded (seedless,
   ruby grapes may be
   substituted)

1. Heat the vegetable oil in a heavy saucepan and add the chicken cut into pieces. Salt and pepper to taste. When nicely browned, add the stock and cinnamon stick. Cover and cook, over moderate heat, for 15 minutes.

2. Whisk together the wine, Curaçao, Maggi, lemon juice, and cornstarch (diluted in the water). Pour over the chicken.

3. Cook, uncovered, until the sauce is creamy and the chicken is done. Remove to heated serving platter and garnish with orange slices and peeled grapes.

Morelia was for many years our retreat. When things got too wild and woolly in the Big City, we'd pack ourselves off to this colonial gem and check into the Posada Villa Montana in Santa María de Güido, overlooking the city.

Proprietor/chef/friend Raymond Coté, started the Posada in the early fifties, when there was just one guest room. Over the years he "grew" it (the only word applicable—he built a room every few months, and often to order—in our case, when there were no open reservations, he built a suite for us for a special anniversary) to a thriving Inn, which hosted world dignitaries for many years.

The hostelry is still thriving today, although not under his gifted hand. Enjoy a dinner there. The view from the terrace is spectacular.

CARNITAS ESTILO BAJÍO

. . . .

Twice Cooked Pork for Tacos

Serves 6

As each region has its own method for preparing beans, so do the recipes for "carnitas" vary. This recipe is inspired by Susana Palazuelos' from Uruapan—delicious and it only soils one pot!

2½ pounds boneless pork
     (fatty cuts are best) cut into 2-inch cubes
8 cups chicken broth
½ large onion
3 whole cloves garlic
2 whole cloves
1 tablespoon coarse salt
1 tablespoon vegetable oil
¾ cup orange juice
½ cup milk

1. In a heavy saucepan or Dutch oven, place the pork, broth, onion, garlic, cloves, and salt. Cover and allow to cook over medium heat for 1½–2 hours or until meat is very tender. Drain the meat, reserving the liquid for gravy or a good soup base.

2. Heat the oil in the same saucepan. Add the orange juice and milk and bring to a low simmer. Add the pork. Cook, uncovered, until all the liquid is absorbed and the meat has browned.

3. Serve with hot tortillas, and *Salsa Verde* (see page 169), to which you have added chopped avocado.

TORTITAS DE EJOTES

Fresh Bean Fritters

Serves 4–6

1 egg + 1 egg white
1 tablespoon olive oil
1 teaspoon vinegar (any variety)
1 teaspoon Dijon-type mustard
½ cup all purpose flour
salt and pepper, to taste
¼ cup milk
1 cup wax beans, cooked to crunch point and chopped
1 cup green beans, cooked to crunch point and chopped
1 small red pepper, chopped fine
½ cup vegetable shortening
salt and pepper, to taste

1. In a medium-size bowl, beat the egg and extra white until fluffy.
2. In a small bowl, whisk together the oil, vinegar, and mustard, and add alternately to the beaten egg, with the flour and salt and pepper.
3. Continue whisking, adding the milk little by little. When the batter is smooth, add the beans and red pepper.
4. Heat the shortening, and drop the batter into it by spoonfuls. Allow the fritters to brown underneath. Turn once, and drain on paper towels. Serve dusted with salt and freshly ground pepper.

The lush farming land around Aguascalientes is the heart of the Bajío. Two of its greatest claims to fame are the museum of the famed political cartoonist, José Guadalupe Posada, and the jewel-like four rooms of the contemporary art museum. The entrance to the latter, which houses the works of native son Saturnino Herrán, is fronted by a magnificent Francisco Zúñiga sculpture.

Dining in the lovely, Porfirian Hotel Francia on the plaza, will always include several fresh vegetable dishes— this confetti-colored combination is one of my favorites, but almost any veggie would be delicious this way.

POLLO DE PLAZA MORELIANA

. . . .

Chicken Morelia-style

Serves 6

2 young chickens, cut into
  serving pieces
3–4 cups chicken broth
6 cloves garlic
1 sprig parsley or thyme
1 large onion, quartered
salt and pepper

Sauce:
½ cup wine vinegar
4 cups water
8 chilies, a combination of
  guajillos, anchos, or pasilla
3 cloves garlic
½ onion
1 teaspoon oregano
salt, to taste
vegetable oil
12 corn tortillas
½ pound Feta cheese,
  crumbled
3 cups cooked carrots, in rounds
24 whole, tiny new potatoes

Garnish:
1 head iceberg lettuce, shredded
1 14-ounce can of tomato sauce (optional)
additional Feta cheese
1 Spanish onion, sliced thin
6 radish roses

I am including this recipe because no chronicle of regional dishes would be complete without it. However, it's difficult for me to conceive that the average cook, with today's busy schedules, would often "whip" this up, although I have simplified the original greatly.

It must also be said that in the late afternoon in Morelia's magnificent, colonial main plaza (the site for much of the action of the '50s Tyrone Power period film, "Captains from Castille"), the aroma of this recipe simmering in dozens of huge copper ollas from nearby Santa Clara del Cobre, is unforgettable and irresistible.

1. Wash and dry the chicken pieces and, in a large, heavy saucepan or skillet with a cover, simmer the pieces with the broth, 6 cloves of garlic, parsley, onion, and salt and pepper, for 30 minutes or until tender.

2. To make the sauce, mix the vinegar and water in a small bowl, add the dried chilies (see pages 181) and soak for 20–30 minutes. Drain and process in a blender with the 3 cloves of fresh garlic, onion, oregano, and salt to taste. Sauté the purée in hot oil for 3 minutes, stirring constantly or it will burn. You may thin with broth if it becomes too thick or dry. Pour the sauce into a large bowl. Do not wash the skillet—set aside.

3. Grease an ovenproof casserole dish. In a separate skillet, heat more lard or vegetable oil. Dip each tortilla in the hot oil, coating both sides. Next, dip each tortilla in the cooked chili sauce, sprinkle with the cheese, fold in half, and keep warm on a heated plate in a 200°F oven.

4. In the sauce skillet, brown the chicken pieces on both sides, adding a little of the chile sauce to give flavor and color. After the chicken is brown, add the carrots and potatoes, and cook for a few more minutes.

5. To serve, prepare a bed of shredded lettuce on a heated platter. Lay out the tortilla halves, slightly overlapping. Top with chicken, carrots, potatoes, and the remains (if any) of the chile sauce. Add tomato sauce if you choose or if it looks too dry. Top with more crumbled Feta cheese, rounds of onion, and garnish with radish roses.

CHILIES

Hot, Hotter, and Hottest

It may come as a great suprise to many of you that of the many "delectables" extant in Mexico today, more than half are not at all hot, in fact, they are completely chili free! Spicy, yes; cumin, coriander, cinnamon, and pepper are used lavishly and usually judiciously (depending on the region and the cook!), but the majority of Mexico's "Haute Cuisine," is flavorful and as much a paradox as the people themselves—it manages to be both subtle and robust at the same time.

The Capsicum or Chili family is indeed however, a main ingredient on the stoves and braziers of the Mexican Indian population. Believed to have medical, magical, and often, aphrodisiac powers (the concept of *machismo* must certainly have come from a chili-eating contest of yore), it is a prime source of flavoring and nutrition for the indigenous masses.

Good friend, Diana Kennedy (to me the supreme authority on Mexican food), notes that there are about 200 different kinds of chilies defined by the botanists; however, only about twenty are common and available in most Mexican produce markets . . . and what a heavenly, nose-twitching presence they are!

Chili, used with moderation, is considered to be a digestive stimulant; unfortunately, restraint is rarely exercised, and the capricious capsicum exits the digestive tract with as much unpleasant "authority" as it enters . . . it can be ferocious! An old Mexican saying translates to:

> *The seeds of machismo are first swallowed*
> *and then descend.*

A glossary of chilies most commonly used in Mexican cuisine

Note: asterisks indicate which few, user-friendly varieties appear in this book.

One of the most "off-putting" qualities in Mexican cooking is a great confusion about the many kinds of chilies. If you want to cook Mexican-style, and the authenticity is less important than the results . . . an exciting and *different* dish, stick with Jalapeños, canned Chipotles, and one of the dried varieties that, after experimentation, you find you like . . . my choice would be the *Guajillo*. Good eating.

FRESH

*Anaheim—(sometimes called California) an American pepper which I use instead of Jalapeños when they are not available). Smooth skinned, bright green, and about 2½ to 3½ inches long. Piquant but rarely palate paralyzing.

*Chile Poblano—A dark green tapering chili, a staple in the Mexican diet. These are used for stuffing *(Chiles Rellenos)* and are also referred to as *rajas* when they are sautéed). These grow to about 8 inches in length and are often quite twisty. Look for the straight ones, they're easier to handle. Their fire ranges from mild to hot.

Güero—The name means "blonde." This is a yellow pepper most often used in Escabeche (see page 268). 4 to 5 inches long. Hot to medium-hot.

*Jalapeño—Everybody's favorite—perhaps because it's the most readily available. Green, smooth skinned, and varying in heat. Measures from 2 to 3 inches.

*Serrano—Bright green and glossy, these little fellers pack a punch. They measure about 1½ to 2½ inches. Watch the seeds!

DRIED

*Ancho—Almost black, short, about 3 inches, and fat (ancho means "wide"), these are dried poblanos. Wrinkled and pliable. These have a fruity flavor and can be very hot.

Arbol—Slender and about 3 inches long. Used for their color and fire. They turn sauces a brilliant orange color. Not for the beginner. Used often in Thai food, too.

*Chipotle—A chocolate brown color,this is the Jalapeño smoked with a distinctive dried chile flavor. When canned they are usually preserved in "adobo" (oil with spices) because they are extremely brittle in their natural state. Can be fiery to mild.

*Guajillo—A popular, wine-colored chili measuring about 4 inches. Mild to medium-hot. I substitute Ancho, when these are not available.

Habañero—(This is called "Scotch Bonnet" in the Caribbean.) Native to the Yucatán, this small (1 x 1-inch), box-shaped variety can be green or orange, althoughm most usually, it is a golden yellow. This is the acetylene torch of chilies, not for the uninitiated.

*Mulato—Often confused with the Guajillo, same specs but a different flavor. Medium-hot.

*Pasilla—A 4- to 6-inch long, black chile. Wrinkled and with an enduring bite. Very popular in sauces.

HOW TO MAKE FRIENDS WITH DRIED CHILIES

Mexicans are very polite. When you meet a Mexican friend, he will first shake hands and then pull you into a bear-like embrace called an *abrazo*, banging both palms on your shoulders.

Las señoras and *las señoritas* vary the "pat down" with kisses into the air, both left and right, cheeks touching. Sometimes you get all three greetings!

The multiphased ceremony is not unlike being introduced to members of the capsicum family. Once you're part of the family however, the taste rewards are endless! Here are a few chile tricks.

- When I'm going to be working with dried chilies, I try to choose a day when my sinuses need aerating—I work with an open window or under the stove extractor, much like I might do when chopping a large amount of onions.
- Wear plastic or rubber gloves and keep your gloved hands away from your mouth and eyes. Capsicum oil can stay on the skin for days and it burns! Now let's get into it:
- Work under running warm water—remove the stem first if you can, and then, with kitchen scissors, split open the chile from one end to the other. Pull out all of the pale membrane and rinse away the seeds. If you're one of the asbestos-palated types, leave some of the seeds in (they're the fire bearers). Dry chilies on paper towels.
- On a hot griddle or in a nonstick fry pan, press down on the chilies with your spatula and "roast," turning often. When they are flat and toasty looking (and your eyes are watering sufficiently), rinse them under hot water, and dry them on a paper towel. Now proceed with your recipe.

If a recipe calls for using fresh chilies (like Poblanos for stuffing), blister them on a hot griddle or fry pan, until they are quite soft and have charred spots over at least half the surface. Immediately place them in a plastic bag, twist the bag tightly shut, and let the chilies cool inside for a few minutes. Now simply rub off the skin (keep those gloves on) and rinse under cold water. Pat dry with paper towels.

If you're going to stuff the chile, cut it lengthwise with the scissors and remove the stem, membranes, and seeds . . . you're ready! Now you can remove your gloves for more delicate work, but be sure to wash your hands with soap and water before you rub an eye or trim a cuticle with your teeth.

JÍCAMA Y NOPALITOS EN VINAGRETA

. . . .

Jícama and Cactus Paddles in Vinaigrette

Serves 4

2 cups jícama, chunked into
   ³/₄-inch cubes
juice of 1 large lemon
6 tablespoons olive oil
3 tablespoons wine vinegar
splash of Maggi
salt and pepper, to taste
1 11-ounce can nopal cactus,
   drained
2 avocados, sliced
4 ripe, plum tomatoes,
   quartered lengthwise
healthy sprig of fresh
   coriander/cilantro
chili powder (for color
   and zip)

Outside of every school in the Republic there is a fruit and vegetable vendor. He sells spears of fresh cucumber, rounds of jícama, and slices of fresh papaya and pineapple. The youngsters tumble out to buy these, topping them with salt and chili powder—truly a lot healthier than candy bars and fries!

It is not generally known, but Mexican families are also cautious with their consumption of fresh greens that are not peeled. To balance this fact, the ingenious Mexican cooks have devised dozens of wonderful salads using cooked vegetables or vegetables which can be peeled. This is one of the best! Working with the fresh cactus is tricky and time consuming, so I suggest you buy it canned.

1. In a medium-sized glass bowl, toss the jícama with the lemon juice and set aside in the refrigerator.

2. Whisk together the oil, vinegar, Maggi, and salt and pepper.

3. On a serving platter, mound the jícama, surrounding it with alternating strips of cactus, avocado, and tomato. Pour the vinaigrette over the vegetables, and garnish with coriander/cilantro and a shake of chili powder.

POSTRE DE MELÓN DE APATZINGÁN

Canteloupe Pudding

Serves 4–6

½ pound almonds, blanched
2 large canteloupes
6 egg yolks
3 cups sugar
1 cup heavy cream, whipped
(optional)

1. Grind the almonds as fine as possible in a minichopper or food processor.
2. Remove and chop the meat of the melon. Blend half the melon and half the ground almonds with the egg yolks and sugar in a large saucepan, and cook over a low flame until the mixture thickens.
3. Fold in the remainder of the melon and almonds, eturn to the flame, and allow, once again, to thicken. Remove from the stove, spoon into individual serving cups, and cool. Serve topped with unsweetened whipped cream, if desired.

The majority of sweet canteloupes that we consume in the United States come from a less-than-sweet-smelling town in Michoacán, México. The rank odor comes from fermenting melons—the legacy of too many, too fast. Melons are a delicate crop, and delay in harvest or shipping can create an olfactory disaster. The locals don't notice it any more and once you've tasted a ripe, heavy melon, warmed from the sun, the supermarket product is a complete turn off!

The recipe comes from San Luís Potosí, but the fruit is from Apatzingán. The dessert is thick, almost paste-like, and a small portion goes a long way. The whipped cream topping makes for total, dessert decadence!

CHISME

PÁTZCUARO

Aren't I the Crafty One?

I collect crafts: no, I'm an incurable craft nut! Whenever the occasion arises to leave the beaten path in search of a copper pot, special tiles, an embroidery typical of the region, or a hand-painted, handwoven, handmade anything, I'm off.

"Where do you want to spend Mother's Day?" Bert asked me. All the kids were away at school and I was beginning to wear that insufferable mantle of "neglected Mom." Good husband was not "having any," so he packed me in the car and we headed for my favorite "goodie hunting ground," the state of Michoacán.

Friday afternoon and Saturday morning were discouragingly barren. We had headed into Santa Clara del Cobre (it has a new, government-type name now, but we still call it by its "right" name, like a familiar old street) to watch the coppersmiths at work, and perhaps add to our collection.

Expecting to see rough-mined copper, visitors are always amazed to see apprentices stripping away the plastic coating of old electrical wire and dropping the red-gold metal shreds into a huge melting pot. The molten copper is poured into a rough mold and cooled, later to be coaxed into a refined shape, hammered, and burnished for sale.

The most exciting bit of theater is when the shop fills an order for a large, round serving tray. At just the right moment in the cooling process, the entire neighborhood gathers, each with his own cloth-covered sledge hammer. A circle is formed around the huge objet d'art-to-be, and at a signal, one of the men gives the tray a hearty "whack" . . . then the next in turn repeats the motion, and so on, until the entire surface is covered in an over-all or specific pattern. This surely is where the anvil chorus originated!

I own one of these gorgeous monoliths of Santa Clara, and it is a jewel, all the more so because I watched its transition from wire to blob to treasure—but that particular day, nothing took my picky fancy, so we headed back towards Pátzcuaro.

On the main drag, Avenida Lázaro Cárdenas, there was (probably still is), a craft shop that wandered through a maze of connected, ramshackle lean-to's. A bargain hunter's paradise . . . a patient husband's nightmare . . . and there it was . . . my mother's day gift!

"Bert, quick, I found it . . . I found it . . . look, look, isn't he beautiful?" Standing on a large, rough-hewn table, covered with dust, was the object of my sudden passion. That it was a "he" was undeniable, this two-thirds, life-size, wooden buffalo was most definitely male . . . anatomically correct in every detail, and splendiferous!

To shorten the anecdote, we haggled with the shopkeeper who told us about the artisan. The craftsman was a Tarascan woodworker from Erongarícuaro, on the other side of the lake. The town is one of the last places in the country that deals in pure barter. Pesos are suspect—they were however, perfectly fine with the merchant who ecstatically rid himself of the huge "bull" in his china shop!

The magnificent sculpture is made from one solid tree, with a hollowed-out section in the beast's back which is hinged to allow you to cache something wonderful in there. We shipped His Highness home, all six hundred pounds of him, and he grazes in a corner of my living room, flanked by a pair of ficus trees, who also seem to think he's just terrific.

CHONGOS ZAMORANOS

. . . .

Little-Knots Milk Dessert

Serves 6

2 egg yolks, beaten
4 cups whole milk, not
    homogenized
2 rennet tablets
1/8 teaspoon salt
2 cups white sugar
2 tablespoons brown sugar
1 2-inch stick cinnamon

1. Beat the egg yolks with a 1/2 cup of milk, and blend in the remaining milk.

2. In the appropriate saucepan (see box above), heat the egg and milk mixture to lukewarm. Blend and strain.

3. Dissolve the rennet tablets and salt in about 3 tablespoons of cold water. Add the milk and egg mixture. Blend well and set in a warm place overnight to form junket.

4. Cut the junket into 2-inch squares or smaller ,if desired. Break up the cinnamon stick and place a sliver of cinnamon in each square. With a spatula, place the squares carefully, one at a time, in a deep saucepan, keeping them separate, and set over a low flame.

5. Dissolve the sugars in 1 cup of water, and when the junket squares begin to bubble, add a cupful of the syrup and the remaining cinnamon. Pour it carefully around the edges of the pan in order not to break the squares. Add more syrup to the junket as pan syrup thickens, until all the syrup has been added. Simmer over very low heat for 1–2 hours, or until the syrup is thick.

6. Allow to cool in the syrup, absorbing the flavor, then refrigerate and serve very cold.

Every culture has its milk-based sweets, starting with Miss Muffet's "curds and whey." Although Chongos are attributed to Zamora, Mexico, its origins are definitely from Spain, and their creamy sweetness is to be found on menus from Monterréy to Mérida.

Caution: You must work with a very low heat, or the "little knots" will separate. I use one of my Mexican clay pots, but a pyrex saucepan over very low heat topped with a heating coil,[1] works well also.

---

[1] Sometimes called a "flame tamer." It is an inexpensive, flat steel coil, available in all kitchen supply and gourmet supply stores.

ATE DE CAMOTE Y PIÑA

. . . .

Sweet Potato and Pineapple Loaf

Yield: 3 1-pound loaves[1]

2 pounds sweet potatoes,
   boiled until tender
1 large can crushed pineapple
2 pounds brown sugar
½ cup liquid

1. Remove the sweet potato skins and all coarse fibers, and purée until smooth in the food processor.

2. Drain the pineapple and reserve the liquid in a measuring cup. Add water if necessary to complete the ½ cup measure of liquid.

3. In a large saucepan or soup pot, heat together the sugar and pineapple liquid, stirring until the sugar is dissolved.

4. Add the sweet potatoes and simmer for 15 minutes, stirring constantly. Add the pineapple and continue to cook slowly, until the mixture is very thick, and the bottom of the pan may be seen when scraped with a spoon.

5. Remove from the heat, divide into 3 parts, and, when cool, mold into 3 oval loaves. Serve sliced on a platter, alternating with slices of fresh cheese.

With wallets happily emptied in the main Plaza (Plaza Gertrudis Bocanegra) and the adjacent Mercado de Ollas (clay pot market), a bargain luncheon was in order. Inquiring of one of the local policia, we trudged up the hill with our bundles, to the Posada San Rafael. The menu was short but ample, and dessert consisted of a slice of this loaf, paired with a slice of a salty, Feta-like cheese—what an inspired combination.

---

[1] When served with cheese, each loaf can serve ten. May also be garnished with chopped almonds and raisins, omitting the cheese.

EL GOLFO

States of:

VERACRUZ,
TAMAULIPAS,
TABASCO

THE GULF:
GLACIERS TO GARDENIAS

When describing the scenic offerings of the three principal gulf states, Tamaulipas, Veracruz, and Tabasco, the paraphrase "when they are good they are very, very good, but when they are bad, they are horrid," applies!

From the spectacular beauty of Mexico's highest peak, Orizaba, and her glistening glaciers, the slope to the Gulf of Mexico is one visual feast after another. Towering pines give way to apple, apricot, and pear orchards, and finally, to the leafy reaches of coffee plantations.

Halfway down, the highway slides into Tehuacán, the home of Mexico's version of designer bottled water, and the hacienda/cum hotel, Fortín de las Flores, famed for its gardenia-filled pools and vast orchid collection.

The city of Veracruz is a study in dilapidated charm and surprising sophistication. As in all ancient ports, the language and physiognomy of its citizens has sprung from the loins of men of the sea; first from Spain, and later, from myriad maritime cultures. Both the patois and the music of merry Veracruz underscore the blend of European, African, and Caribbean melding.

The cuisine of the City of the Bamba is also a happy mixture of the best of many distant and exotic kitchens, seasoned with Mexican creativity and supplied by the largesse of the Gulf. *Huachinango a la Veracruzano* (Red snapper Veracruz-style) may be found on fine menus all over the world.

* * * *

Hugging the coastline northbound will frustrate and disappoint you. The reason—economics—Mexico's principal export, crude oil, is badgered out of the earth all the way from Veracruz to Tampico. The ugly metal structures of the industry: towering rigs, burn-off stacks, and the mesmeric steel grasshopper rigs nod for miles of shoreline.

The Mexico of the Gulf, which has beauty to spare, lies south. Hurry through industrial Lerdo, to begin to savor what Patricia Quintana calls, in her beautiful book, *A Taste of Mexico*, the home of the nation's "dessert ingredients." Vanilla, coffee, and banana plantations abound. Fields of fat watermelons and stands of papaya and mango trees prosper under the warm sun and gulf breezes. Tobacco, for the pungent, after-dinner cigars of San Andrés Tuxtla, is also grown here.

Stop to stretch in the battered village of Alvarado, the home of Mexico's most inventive and graphic curse words; spin through Tlacotalpan with its pastel porticoes, and, if it is January, rent a room with a balcony on the main plaza for the safe witness of the, "Pamplona-like," free running of the bulls. Now on to the volcanic glories of the Tuxtlas (Santiago Tuxtla and San Andrés Tuxtla) and misty Catemaco, with its magnificent lake.

The cuisine of the Gulf as expected, underlines the natural wealth of the warm Gulf waters: oysters, crab, shrimp, and langoustines, snowy pompano, red snapper, luscious grouper, and the now popular firm-fleshed shark. (Speaking of shark, the gentle surf of the Gulf invites, but please swim only where the tattered lines of shark nets are visible. The streamlined predators like the Veracruz menus too!)

The citrus groves, while perfuming the air, also supply the region with its most popular recipe ingredient and garnish. Mexican limes, called *limones*, are omnipresent, and are used as an integral seasoning for everything from chicken broth to seafood. The use of vinegar is popular, and the Mexican vinaigrette (*escabeche*), may be found on every table in small dishes, to be used as a relish, or simply enjoyed with a fresh *bolillo* (French roll), or fragrant, hot tortilla, while waiting for the next course.

Tiny Tabasco, the gateway to Mayaland, is a giant in terms of the yield of its rich earth. *Cacao*, spiny pineapples, chestnuts and other nuts, and dozens of varieties of the chilies, so integral a part of the delicious Mexican table, share acreage with grazing livestock and Olmec ruins.

THINGS TO SEE, DO, AND EAT

Villahermosa: Enjoy the orchids and tame deer grazing in the Parque La Venta which showcases several dozen Olmec treasures, including monolithic stone heads and many jaguar-depicting sculptures and mosaics. Sip a glass of cool *horchata* (a melon seed or rice-based beverage), refreshingly sweet and nonalcoholic. Tabascan dishes to try: *Sopa de Mariscos* (a spicy seafood chowder), *Acamaya al Ajillo* (a kind of freshwater crayfish smothered in garlic and oil), and the local fish, *pejelagarto*, shredded with chilies, limes, and served with hot tortillas as an appetizer.

Veracruz: Pre-Lenten Carnaval is celebrated here in a big way! Home of the *Bamba* and the *Son*; regional dances, the first merrily raucous and the second, insidiously sensual. Don't miss the Sunday evening outdoor dances at the Parque Ciriaco Vasques— the combination of Spain, Africa, and Cuba makes for torrid performing, with the de rigueur, dead-pan faces and heated hips. In suburban Boca del Rio, waterfront cafes and open-to-the-beach restaurants serve local seafood specialties.

Papantla: A good native market to buy whole vanilla beans and the loose, white cotton shirts and trousers worn by the Totonacs (chic for hot weather casual wear).

El Tajín: Home of the Pyramid of the Niches, a wedding-cake-like ruin whose origins are cloudy. It is known that Huastecs, Otomís, Olmecs, and Totonacs all inhabited the site during different eras, but the architecture bears the Mayan stamp—mysterious and quite wonderful.

Jalapa: An arts center dubbed the Athens of Mexico, punctuated with lovely old Colonial mansions, a fine anthropology museum, myriad coffee shops in which to enjoy the wonderful coffee of the region, and peek-a-boo looks at the snowy summit of the volcano, Citlaltépetl. Carry a sweater—it gets nippy in the afternoons and evenings.

Tlacotalpan: A poor man's Pamplona in January, bulls careen through the streets to be tested by every aspiring *torero*.

San Andrés Tuxtla: Home of the Mexican cigar, Tabacos San Andrés.

Catemaco: Known for fresh water snails, *tegagolos*, dredged from the lake and served like our shrimp cocktail with a hot, tomato sauce.

Tampico: Fish, fish, and more fish—eat your fill, it's fresh!

Ciudad Madero: The Huastec Museum in the Tecnológico Madero is a must for archeology buffs.

LINGUISTIC GARNI

Language is a trap for Americans. The accent and dialect of certain regions of Mexico can confuse and stupefy. The most confounding jargons come from the ports, where language has been colored and bastardized by the infusion of many cultures.

The patois of the Gulf states owes much of its unintelligiblity to the early Cuban travelers, who came across the Gulf and stayed. Final consonants are dropped or swallowed entirely, and to the unaccustomed, the speech rhythms often seem to be played at double speed!

To further complicate this, no matter how proficient we become in the Latin-rooted languages, the nuances of the (*tu*) familiar, and the more formal (*usted*), lie ever at bushwacking "ready." The romance-language, grammatical fact is that the pronoun *su* meaning *your* also translates to: *his*, *hers*, and *its*.

One day while training a new arrival from Veracruz to serve the table, I painstakingly emphasized that the garnish, in this case, parsley, should be arranged at the last moment in the mouth of the gorgeous, whole red snapper we were to serve.

The instruction went like this:

Antes de llevar el pescado a la mesa, pon un manojo de perejíl en su boca. Translation: *Before bringing the fish to the table put a sprig of parsley in "its" mouth.*

The rosy fish arrived in the dining room, steaming and fragrant with herbs and Jalapeño peppers. The platter on which it reposed was borne triumphantly by Antonieta, our new employee, who with stately pace, arrived with a huge mouthful of fresh parsley clenched firmly in her teeth!

So much for the vagaries of language and the niceties of *garde manger*.

OSTIONES PUERTO CEIBA

Oysters with Tequila

Serves 4

Oysters fresh from the sea offer a briny but neutral base for many sauces. Try this specialty of Puerto Ceiba in Tabasco, seated cozily in your mind, on the edge of Laguna Mecoacán.

1 head garlic, peeled and minced fine
8 tablespoons light olive oil
12 fresh tortillas, cut into julienne ribbons (see below)
4 dozen fresh oysters
½ cup white tequila
salt, if desired

1. Lightly brown the garlic in the olive oil. Toss well with the tortilla ribbons until well coated.
2. Shuck the oysters and loosen the muscle, keeping the oyster in the half shell. Heat the oven to 475°F.
3. Top the oysters with the tortilla ribbons and pour about 2 tablespoons of tequila over each topped oyster.
4. Place the filled shells in a baking casserole (use kosher salt around the shells to steady them if necessary), and bake for 10 minutes. Serve at once with kosher salt on the side.

SOPA DE CAMARONES JAROCHA

Shrimp Soup, Veracruz-style

Serves 6

2 tablespoons vegetable oil
2 tomatoes, peeled, chopped, and squeezed dry
2 large onions, chopped fine
2 cloves garlic, chopped fine
¼ cup blanched almonds, chopped
¼ cup prunes, cooked, pitted, and diced
¼ cup seedless raisins
1 teaspoon allspice
2 teaspoons chopped parsley
1 cup stock (more for a thinner soup)
1 teaspoon salt
2 pounds medium-sized shrimp, peeled and chopped
1 cup scalded milk
croutons

Jarochas *is the name given to the natives of irreverant Veracruz, the merriest of all of Mexico's populous. Added to their unique sense of humor is the combined Latin and African-influenced music, which combines the hops and heel taps of the Bamba, with the pelvis-grinding beat of the Danzón.*

All of this furious activity builds an appetite. Veracruz is the Boston of Mexico, in that it is the only region where milk is added to seafood chowders and stews. This fruited version came to notice in Túxpan one sultry evening, sitting at a plaza table and watching the local teenagers flirt and strut.

1. Heat the oil in a large skillet, add the tomatoes, onions, and garlic, and sauté for several minutes over low heat.
2. Add the almonds, prunes, and raisins, and sauté for 8–10 minutes more. Add the allspice and parsley and cook a few minutes longer.
3. In a large saucepan, heat the stock and salt, and simmer for a few minutes. Add the seasoned fruit mixture and let simmer for 5 minutes until all the flavors are melded.
4. Now add the raw shrimp and simmer 3–4 minutes longer. Put some of this mixture in each soup plate and top with a little hot milk. Garnish with croutons.

CHILPACHOLE DE CANGREJO

Crab Soup, Veracruz-style

Serves 6

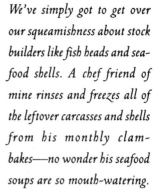

We've simply got to get over our squeamishness about stock builders like fish heads and seafood shells. A chef friend of mine rinses and freezes all of the leftover carcasses and shells from his monthly clambakes—no wonder his seafood soups are so mouth-watering.

This soup, when made in Veracruz, involves splashing and mashing and good-natured cussing. When I make it, I cuss less, but the splashing and mashing come with the territory. The results are worth it!

4 tablespoons olive oil
1 medium-sized onion, chopped
3 garlic cloves, mashed
1 bell pepper, chopped
8 cups clam juice
2 carrots, chopped
3 stalks celery, leave greens attached
1 teaspoon dried oregano
¼ cup fresh coriander/cilantro, chopped
2 chipotle chilies (canned are fine) rinsed and seeded
4 ripe tomatoes, peeled and chopped
6 medium-sized crabs (blue if possible, if not, substitute 3 large Dungeness)

1. In large skillet heat the oil. Sauté the onion, garlic, and bell pepper until soft.

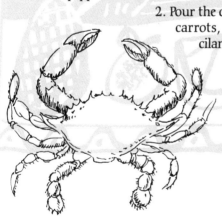

2. Pour the clam juice into a soup pot with the carrots, celery, oregano, and coriander/cilantro. Slow boil until the vegetables are tender. Add the chipotle chilies and the sautéed onion, garlic, bell pepper, and tomatoes. Continue at a slow boil for about 20 minutes.

3. Pop the crabs into the pot and cover. Simmer for about 5 minutes or until the crabs turn red. Remove the crabs from pot and, working carefully (they're hot!), remove the legs and pull back the apron of each crab (see below). This allows the broth to get into the body of the crab, and also to be flavored more intensely. Return the bodies and legs to pthe ot, cover, and continue cooking for another 15 minutes.

4. Remove the crabs from the soup and extract the meat. Divide the meat among 6 deep bowls and add the vegetables and the crab legs. Cover with the broth. Serve with wedges of lemon and hot tortillas.

SOPA TABASQUEÑA

Tabasco-style Soup

Serves 6

1 cup of rice
½ teaspoon saffron powder
1 egg
¼ teaspoon salt
2 tablespoons seedless raisins
4 tablespoons orange juice
3 tablespoons vegetable oil
2 cloves garlic, chopped
1 small onion, chopped
1 medium-sized tomato,
  chopped
1 sweet pepper, seeded, and
  chopped
1 teaspoon capers
12 green olives, chopped
1 sweet potato, cooked and chopped
2 bananas, sliced
2 hard-cooked eggs, chopped
2 medium-sized white potatoes, boiled, peeled, and chopped
olive oil

The second week in May, the Usamacinta River Marathon is run in Villahermosa. This regional sopa seca (dry soup) could well be the Mexican version of pre-race carbohydrate loading! Runner or not, this is delicious as a side dish for pork or poultry, or makes a nice light supper served with a green salad.

For those nutritionists among you, it is not unusual in Mexico to find rice and potatoes in the same dish.

1. Cook the rice, covered, in 2 cups of water, with the saffron powder. Beat the egg with the salt and stir into the rice.

2. Soak the raisins in the orange juice.

3. Heat the vegetable oil in a medium-sized skillet, and sauté the garlic, onion, tomato, sweet pepper, plumped raisins, capers, olives, sweet potato, banana, and hard-cooked eggs.

4. Put a layer of half the rice in the bottom of a buttered baking dish. Then add a layer of the sautéed ingredients. Cover with the remaining rice and the chopped white potatoes. Drizzle with olive oil. Bake in a hot oven at 425°F for 15 minutes or until the potatoes are browned.

ENSALADA DE AGUACATE, FRUTAS Y PIÑON

Avocado, Fruit, and
Pine Nut Salad

In cultivation, two of the most beautiful of Mexico's tropical crops are the pineapple and the avocado. The ordered rows of the spiny fruit say tropics *to the viewer, and the shade of the magnificent avocado trees is welcomed.*

Serves 6

2 cups pineapple chunks (fresh ripe or canned)
3 ripe avocados (the black Haas variety have the most flavor)
2 tablespoons lemon juice or juice from the canned pineapple
2 oranges, peeled and sectioned
1 tablespoon wine vinegar
3 tablespoons brown sugar
¼ cup Marsala or sweet sherry
¼ cup pine nuts, toasted lightly

1. If you are using canned pineapple, reserve the juice to acidulate (keep from turning brown) the avocado chunks, or use the lemon juice.
2. Lightly toss the pineapple chunks, avocado, and orange segments with the vinegar, brown sugar, and wine. Spoon into serving bowls and garnish with pine nuts.

FRIJOLES CON PLÁTANO MACHO

Beans with Bananas

Serves 4

3 ripe macho bananas
3 tablespoons melted butter
3 tablespoons all-purpose flour
1/3–1/2 cup vegetable
   shortening (additional if
   needed)
1 cup cooked beans of your
   preference (I like the red
   beans)
sour cream
nutmeg

1. Mash the bananas well, incorporating the butter and flour to make a stiff batter.

2. Heat 1 tablespoon of shortening in a medium-sized skillet and quick-fry the beans for 5 minutes. Mash them with a fork, and turn the flame down to low while you cook the batter.

3. In a deep-sided griddle or skillet, melt the rest of the shortening, and drop tablespoonsful of the batter into the hot fat, flattening each cake into a 3-inch diameter circle. Fry for several minutes until brown underneath, and turn the "pancake" over to brown on the other side.

4. Serve topped with a tablespoon of fried beans (see page 28) and a dollop of sour cream sprinkled with nutmeg.

There are at least four varieties of bananas sold in the wholesale produce markets of Mexico. The golden variety, with which we are most familiar, is called plátano Tabasco; *an entire bunch of* dominicos *is the size of your hand, and they are said to be the most digestible for babies and convalescents. The fat, sweet* morados *are dark red in hue while the large, tough,* machos *are called* plantains *in other parts of Latin America, and are used only for cooking. Allow the outside skin of the machos to turn black before using, otherwise they are stringy and unpleasant tasting.*

CHILES RELLENOS CON SARDINAS

Chilies Stuffed with Sardines

Serves 4

This dish from Tuxpan is traditionally prepared with spicy Chiles Poblanos, but because they are often not available outside of Mexico, I've recreated the dish with the zing in the filling, rather than the "container."

Large sardines, canned in a mild tomato sauce, are a Mexican pantry staple.

4 large green peppers
1 tablespoon olive oil
½ large Spanish onion, chopped fine
2 4½-ounce cans sardines in tomato sauce
½ cup Chihuahua cheese (white Cheddar)
¼ teaspoon dried oregano
8 large green olives, chopped
2 canned Jalapeño chilies, rinsed, deveined, seeded, and minced (optional)
juice of 2 limes
salt and pepper, to taste

Batter:
2 eggs separated
2 tablespoons all-purpose flour
pinch of baking powder
pinch of salt

1. Wash the peppers. Remove the stem, core, and seeds. Parboil them for about 10 minutes.
2. Heat the oil and sauté the onion. Mash the sardines with their sauce. (It is not necessary to skin or debone sardines.)
3. Mix the onion and sardines with the cheese, oregano, olives, chilies, and lime juice. Spoon the filling into the peppers and set aside.
4. Prepare the batter by beating the egg yolks. Then, in a separate bowl, beat the egg whites until they form peaks. Fold together with the flour, baking powder, and salt.
5. Dip the peppers in this batter and fry in deep fat until puffed and golden brown. Drain on paper towels and serve at once with a flavored tomato sauce on the side.

CACTI

A Prickly Subject

The land stretches and bunches into little hills, much like an army of inch worms randomly pursuing whatever it is that inch worms pursue. The vista is broken by jutting stands of cacti, both the *magueyes* planted as boundaries between *ejidos* (land parcels) and the globular-leaved *nopales*.

The cactus in Mexico embodies what is rudimentary—the basic earthiness . . . the He-She complicity for survival . . . the strength against odds, the God will, and the passionate sensuality.

What we know as the Century Plant, the *Maguey*, is an ancient symbol of masculinity; in bloom its waxy phallus is visible for miles around. Before its pre-Death blossoming, its deep, blue-green spikes are a source of life to the Indians who tend it.

- The leaves are used for cooking utensils; acting as curved receptacles for the savory mixtures to be steamed. They are also wet and dried, and then woven into an infinite number of objects, useful and often quite beautiful.
- The spines become primitive sewing implements and the ravelled edges of the *maguey* are used to stitch together placemats and basket seams.
- The heart bestows a semen-like life fluid *pulque*— as it ferments, a source and surcease from the pain of encroaching civilization.

The *Nopal* (g. *opuntia*) is more familiar to us. Like a fistfull of green balloons, each rounded-leaf sprouts another until finally a rosy bloom gives birth to the fruit (*tuna*); spiny but sweet . . . we call it a prickly pear.

In shape and destiny, the *Nopal* is the feminine force in Mexico's nature, the nurturer. All of Mexico's landscape boasts these "families," *maguey* and *nopal* . . . co-existing, crowding, multiplying, invading . . . their very fertility in the rocky, hardpan of the high plateau, a nose-thumbing by Mother Nature.

In the culinary context, the only cactus with which we need to deal is the *nopal*. Most ethnic food stores sell them by the leaf, and with thought for the consumer, they even de-spine them. If you plan to use your own backyard variety, I suggest you pick them with leather-palmed gloves and bring them into the kitchen sink for a good rinse. Still gloved, scrape off the spines with a potato peeler or short, sharp knife and wash all of the little spiny nasties down into the garbage grinder. They have a pervasive way of eluding even the sharpest eyes, and end up happily festering in your unhappy thumb.

Don't ever reach for a prickly pear with a bare hand—ouch, ouch, and ouch! The Indians in Mexico remove the spines imbedded in flesh by heating a wax candle and spreading the tallow over the puncture or punctures, letting the wax sit for a moment to penetrate the pores, and then peeling off the wax with the spines.

Cut the now-harmless leaves into smallish pieces (about one-half inch) and boil them in salted water until they are fork tender. Rinse with cold water to remove the slippery residue and proceed as the recipe requires. What do they taste like? A cross between a string bean and the slightly acrid bite of a dandelion leaf. Addictive!

TORTA TAMPIQUEÑA DE CAMARÓN

Shrimp Omelet Tampico-style

Serves 4

All sizes of shrimp are har-vested from the deep waters of the Gulf of Mexico. The small shrimp we call "Angel shrimp" that are so delicious in salads, are perfect for this simple brunch or supper recipe.

4 tablespoons vegetable oil
1 cup scallions, chopped, with the tender half of the
    green stem
1 cup sweet red pepper, chopped
1 Jalapeño pepper, seeded, deveined, and chopped fine (optional)
3 cups Swiss chard or fresh spinach, washed and torn into
    2-inch pieces
½ teaspoon oregano
salt and pepper, to taste
½–¾ pound small shrimp, steamed and shelled
8 eggs, beaten

1. In a 12- or 14-inch iron skillet, heat the oil and sauté the scal-lions, sweet pepper, and Jalapeño chile until limp.
2. Add the chard or spinach (you may use a package of frozen, but drain well) and seasonings. Stir until the fresh greens are limp and the flavors are melded.
3. Fold in the shrimp and spread the ingredients evenly over the bottom of the pan. Add the beaten eggs, and allow the omelet to set, pulling the edges away from the skillet with a knife or spatula.
4. Cover and cook until the top is set.
5. Cut into fourths and serve on heated plates garnished with lemon wedges and parsley.

SOPA SECA DE PLÁTANO

Banana Soup

Serves 6

10 red-skinned, under-ripe
    bananas or plantains
2 cups orange juice
1/4 teaspoon cloves
1/4 teaspoon orégano
1 teaspoon powdered
    cinnamon
salt, to taste
4 tablespoons vegetable oil

Sauce:
4 medium-sized tomatoes,
    peeled, chopped, and drained
2 green peppers, chopped
1 medium-sized onion, grated
1/4 cup olive oil
1 teaspoon salt
splash of hot sauce or Tabasco

Forget the romantic strains of "Tampico, Tampico, on the gulf of Mexico," there is little romantic about the bustling oil town honored by the song.

The best part of the city is a fine museum of Huastec Art to be found in the Tecnológico Madero and a taste of this unlikely "soup." It falls into the category of "dry" soups and makes an unusual sweet/savory side dish for poultry or pork. The recipe was wheedled out of a waiter (with charm and a large tip) at the Colonial Hotel, near the Plaza.

1. In a large skillet, cook the unpeeled bananas or plantains in water to cover, over low heat for about 10 minutes. Remove the bananas, add the orange juice and simmer, allowing it to boil down to about one-half cup of liquid.

2. Peel the bananas and mash with the cloves, oregano, cinnamon, orange juice, and a pinch of salt. Heat the oil and sauté the banana mixture until slightly browned. Divide into serving bowls and top with the tomato sauce.

3. To prepare the sauce, heat the oil and sauté the tomatoes, peppers, and onion for about 5 minutes over moderate high heat. Salt to taste.

CARNE HUASTECA

Beef, Huastec-style

Serves 8

4–5 pounds fillet of beef, in
  1 piece
2 medium-sized heads of garlic
  cloves, separated
2 tablespoons of freshly
  ground black pepper
2 tablespoons ground allspice
½ teaspoon each of ground
  cloves and cinnamon
1 teaspoon cumin seeds,
  ground
2 tablespoons dried oregano
orange juice or cider vinegar
salt, to taste

The Huastec civilization was active over a thousand years ago. A prickly folk (certainly from the point of view of the Aztecs with whom they were constantly at war), their modern-day descendants, prepare this version of the classic carne asada. The "rub" used here owes much to the Yucatecan Recados (see page 260) and acts not only to season but also to seal in the juices of the meat. I have tried to adapt some of the native ingredients to what most of us find in our American pantries.

1. Shape (or have your butcher do it) the fillet until it looks like a fat salami and tie it to hold its shape.

2. Roast the garlic by spreading the unpeeled cloves in a nonstick fry pan over medium heat, moving the cloves frequently. When they are soft and slightly blackened, slip the skins off the cloves and discard. Mash the pulp.

3. Make a *recado* by mixing the garlic with the pepper, allspice, cloves, cinnamon, cumin, and oregano. Add enough orange juice or vinegar to make a heavy paste. Rub the fillet well, using all of the *recado*. Place in a roasting pan and let sit at room temperature to season, for about 30 minutes.

4. Heat oven to 475°F. Place the fillet on a rack and roast for 5 minutes, then lower heat to 375°F for about 25 minutes. The meat thermometer should read 130°F for rare meat.

5. Slice across the meat in 1-inch thick diagonals. Traditionally served with hot tortillas, *Guacamole* (see page 25), an individual ball of mozzarella cheese (most similar to the mild cheese of the Huastec region), and a serving of *Frijoles de Olla* (see page 251) . . . or eat it with whatever you please . . . it's delicious!

TERNERA ESTILO TABASQUEÑO

Veal, Tabasco-style

Serves 4

4 4–6-ounce boneless veal
    cutlets
½ teaspoon coarse salt
¾ cup beef stock
¼ teaspoon each, white
    pepper and dried marjoram
1 pinch each ground cumin
    and ground cloves
several strands of saffron
    (optional)
4 cloves garlic, minced
2 tablespoons vegetable oil
1 sweet red pepper, chopped
1 medium-sized onion,
    chopped fine
3 medium-sized tomatoes,
    peeled and chopped
3 hard-cooked eggs
1 tablespoon butter or margarine
1 tablespoon mild vinegar

Tabasco's abundance of fresh waterways (rivers, lakes, and picture-book lagoons) make it prime grazing land for some of the best beef the Republic has to offer. Young beef is called becerro, *while the veal to which we are accustomed is called* ternera, *or* ternera chica, *depending on the age of the calf.*

This recipe clearly shows the multicultural roots of the coast in its use of widely varying seasoning. Note the use of cooked egg yolks as a thickening agent for the fragrant sauce, and the vinegar which is a recurring element in Gulf flavoring.

1. Pound each cutlet well to flatten and tenderize. Cut each cutlet into 4 pieces. Place in heavy 2- to 3-quart saucepan. Sprinkle lightly with salt.

2. Pour one-half cup of stock over the veal and add the herbs, spices, and 1 clove of the minced garlic. Allow to simmer for 15 minutes.

3. In a large skillet, heat the oil and sauté the red pepper, onion, tomatoes, and the remaining garlic. Pour over the meat, cover, and continue simmering until the sauce is no longer a soupy consistency and the meat is tender.

4. Into a mixing bowl, sieve the egg yolks and blend with the remaining stock. Add to the meat mixture alternately with the melted butter and the vinegar. Cook over medium heat for 6–10 minutes. Adjust the seasoning, adding salt if necessary.

I serve this with white rice and a large accompanying plate of fresh watercress which abounds in the Tabascan rivers and streams. Squeeze a lemon over the cress and season with salt and pepper.

CONEJO EN MOLE CAMPESTRE

Rabbit in Country "Mole"

Serves 4–6

Sauce for 4 pounds
of cooked rabbit,[1]
cut into serving pieces:
8 dried ancho chiles
1 pound ripe tomatoes, peeled
3 cloves garlic
1 cup almonds, blanched and
    fine ground (will measure
    about ½ cup)
⅓ cup raisins
1 large "plantain" banana
    (or 2 slightly underripe
    regular bananas)
4 slices whole grain bread
3 tablespoons brown sugar
1 teaspoon of mixed ground
    cloves, cinnamon, and black
    pepper in equal amounts
⅓ cup vegetable oil
2 squares unsweetened baking
    chocolate
chicken broth, to the desired
    consistency
salt, to taste
¼ cup sesame seeds

Papantla, Veracruz is the home of the world famous Indios Voladores (*Flying Indians*). These descendents of the Totonacs were doing their version of bungee jumping before the Aussies ever dreamt about the sport.

Dressed in dunce-shaped hats, embroidered red cotton trousers, loose white shirts, and black, high-heeled boots, five religious daredevils scale a 100-foot pole to a saucer-like platform from which four of them hurl themselves headfirst out into space. While they spiral around the pole and each other, in widening concentrics to honor Tonatiúh, the Sun God, the fifth "dancer" plays a haunting recorder solo to the God. If you can bear to watch until the end, they continue to defy the ground until the last moment, when in unison, they somersault upright—it's agonizing yet riveting to watch.

Wild rabbit is a delicacy of the environs, sometimes grilled over a brazier with quantities of fresh oregano and marjoram. On feast days it is served in this exquisite sauce—Tonatiúh must have been quite the gourmand!

[1] This *mole* is equally savory on poultry and game meats.

1. Working with rubber gloves, sear, peel, and devein the chilies. In a small saucepan, cover the chilies with water and allow to boil for a minute or 2. Remove from the heat, cover, and set aside.
2. Squeeze out the seeds and excess juice from the tomatoes and coarse grind them in the food processor with the garlic. Add the almonds, raisins, banana, bread, sugar, and spices. Blend together until you have a grainy paste.
3. Pour into large skillet in which you have heated the oil. Sauté at a bubble for a few minutes, allowing the flavors to meld. Remove from the stove, cover, and set aside.
4. Drain the chilies and dry on a paper towel. In another very lightly oiled skillet, "toast" the chilies until they begin to curl. Add to the tomato mixture and sauté for 5 more minutes. Remove from the heat. Allow to cool sufficiently to be able to purée to a smooth paste consistency.
5. Dissolve the chocolate in the broth and add to the chilies and tomatoes, stirring constantly. Add more broth as needed until the *mole* is gravy thick and satiny. Taste to adjust for sugar and salt. **Neither flavor should overpower the other**. Pour over the rabbit pieces and garnish with sesame seeds.

BEVERAGES

"Salud, Amor y Pesetas"

Mexico is a thirsty country—the rationale of course being that much of it is very hot, either tropical humid or desert dry, both of which dehydrate. The truth is that the holding of a glass, filled with anything from fruit juice to something fermented or distilled, telegraphs pleasure.

Don the unbleached muslin trousers of a laborer, toiling in the fields or helping build one of Mexico's remarkable skyscrapers, what is your most pleasurable thought—a brief rest and a *refresco* (cold drink).

No calloused hands yours, you're a salaried bureaucrat, pushing papers in an ill-lit office—Oh, for that coffee break— *cafe con leche* and a sweet roll are definitely on your mind.

Mr. R. A. Tycoon—lunch at the club with clients and a tequila with lemon and salt on the web of your thumb, and then wine with the meal and cogñac with coffee—it's the M.O. of big business.

Students, workers, housekeepers, employed, or unemployed, chances are that several times a day, you're going to stop and *tomar algo* (drink something).

Pushcarts abound to satisfy the national thirst.

Fruit juices mixed with water, like lemon- or orangeades, glow in huge glass barrels; *licuados* made from concentrated extracts of fruits and vegetables are hawked by the proud owner of a *licuador* as he forces, carrots, celery, and tomatoes down the maw of the noisy little machine.

Of the drinks native to Mexico, the most basic is *pulque*.

In the fields you still see a phenomenon called the *Tlachiquero*. His employ is an ancient one—taking a huge gourd, chosen for its shape and size, he inserts it into the hollowed out heart of the maguey cactus and sucks out the collected, *agua miel* (honey water), which is then trans-ferred to another carrying gourd usually tied to the wooden saddle of his burro. This sweetish *pulque* ferments at an amazing rate and is drunk either straight or *curado* (mixed with fruit juice). It was at one time available everywhere, one ambitious manufacturer even tried canning it.

Mescal and tequila (please **don't** pronounce it *te-quee-ya*—it only has one "l.") are first cousins, the former being sort of the poor relation, not quite as polished or groomed. Tequila is the successful member of the family, big business indeed. Tequila, like other fine spirits, comes in several quali-ties, and can range from smooth as silk (some of the *añejos*, aged) to the bite of a bullwhip. The amber hue of the more expensive añejos has less to do with time in the barrel and more to due with a brown sugar additive. I'm a purist and a plebeian and like Cuervo Blanco Suave and Hornitos Blanco . . . I like the odd taste of the cactus and don't want it soft-ened or obliterated!

Mezcal is the infamous drink with the little bag of worm and chili powder attached. The accompanying edible mag-got doesn't bother me as much as the oily viscosity of the drink itself, but then "to each his own!"

In taquerías everywhere, fruit beers are sold, *Tepache* being one of the most popular, it's sweet-sour taste an effec-tive quencher. Speaking of beer, Mexican beers give no quar-

211
EL GOLFO

ter to the Europeans. *Negra Modelo* is a heavy (a bit like Stout), dark brew, as is the *Tres Equis* (*xxx*) and the delicious *Nochebuena* or Christmas beer.

Light beers, some of which can be used to delicious results in recipes in these pages, include: *Dos Equis*, *Bohemia*, *Superior* (an advertising campaign christened it *La Rubia de Categoría*, the blonde with class, and used a bosomy blond, cinema sex symbol as their trademark), *Corona* and *Carta Blanca*. *Tecate* was the beer bought by the U.S. navy during WW II.

Mexican wines, although they've come a long way, are still lacking in polish and finish. Two of the better labels are: Hidalgo, and Santo Tomás.

Baja California is bottling an impressive Cabernet Sauvignon from Monte Xanic, $16–$18, pricey for a Mexican wine, but worth it. Less expensive, try the L. A. Cetto Nebbiolo '85 or '87, with a respectable fruitiness and a developing deep finish for its $7–$8.

My choice for complementing wines is California's product. The slightly higher alcohol content, fruitiness, and climactic influence of the Pacific and the rocky belt of the Santa Lucia mountains, make for a happy marriage with the exotic and spicy cuisine of Mexico.

Some of the marvelous beverages offered in regional Mexico are:

COLD

- **Tepache:** a low alcohol "beer" made from pineapple

- **Horchata:** A milky drink made from ground almonds, melon seeds or cooked rice. (See page 244) Note: Recipe varies according to the region.

- **Agua de Tamarindo:** an infusion of tamarind pods, sugar, and water

- **Agua de Jamaica:** a "tea" made from the calyxes of a tropical blossom

- **Chía:** Chía seeds are what grow in the little clay figures of animals and heads to make amusing green "hair" or "wool." A refreshing lemonade is made with the seeds which swell, creating an interesting texture.
- **Licuados:** milk, chipped ice, and fresh, ripe fruit whirred in the blender

HOT:

- **Cafe de olla:** Mexican coffee flavored with brown sugar and cinnamon, served in a clay pot.
- **Atole:** A corn masa beverage, almost like a thin gruel, flavored with brown sugar (or molasses), chocolate or spices or fruits or a combination. Said to be a cure for everything!
- **Chocolate caliente:** hot chocolate made from a cinnamon-flavored block of chocolate, melted, blended with milk or water, and then aerated with a carved wooden "Molinillo" (mill) to produce abundant foam

What should you say when you raise your glass? The most common toast is:

"Salud, amor y pesetas y tiempo para gozarlas."
"Health, love, and money and time to enjoy them."

Salud, all by itself is sufficient, however. Do touch glasses though, a mere raising of the glass is considered bad luck or at best, an insincerity.

PESCADO VERACRUZANA

Fish, Veracruz-style

Serves 6

The venerable Hotel Mocambo shows the ravages of the salty Gulf air, but we might say she is ageing gracefully. This recipe is a modernization of a recipe I coaxed from the hotel chef over 30 years ago. As with many recipes of the region, the ingredients list is long, but the preparation quick and easy, and the results are lip-smacking.

6 4–6-ounce fillets of a firm, white fish (halibut, haddock, cod, shark)
½ medium-sized onion, diced
1 clove garlic, minced fine
¼ cup vegetable or mild olive oil
2 cups prepared tomato sauce
1–2 tablespoons chili powder, or to taste
2 peppercorns, cracked
¼ teaspoon cinnamon
2 pinches ground cloves
½ teaspoon sugar
1 tablespoon lemon juice
3 small red potatoes, boiled, peeled, and cubed
18 green olives, pimento stuffed
toast triangles

1. In a heavy saucepan, sauté the onion and garlic in half of the oil until transparent. Add the tomato sauce and spices, and stir until the flavors have melded, about 3 minutes.

2. Blend in the sugar and lemon juice, adding water if the sauce is too thick.

3. In a large skillet (preferably nonstick), heat the remaining oil and panfry the fish fillets. Add the potatoes to the pan. Pour the sauce over the fish and potatoes, and continue to simmer for about 3 minutes.

4. Carefully transfer to a heated platter, garnishing with the olives and toast triangles. Serve at once.

PONCHE COSTEÑO

Coastal Drink

Yield: 6 servings

1 cup water
1¾ cups sugar
1 2-inch cinnamon stick
1 cup pineapple juice
1 cup orange juice
2 shots brandy (optional)
2 cups white wine
1 can crushed pineapple
chopped ice

Because Mexico is tropical, the coastal regions can be Hades hot! This delicious, slightly alcoholic "refresco" is made with boiled water, so "No worries, amigo."

When in the tropics, remember to drink more than your usual intake of liquids, or you may suffer a dehydration headache or light headedness.

1. In a medium-sized saucepan, boil the water, sugar, and cinnamon over low heat for 5 minutes. Cool. Remove the cinnamon stick.
2. Strain the fruit juices and add to a bowl containing the brandy, wine, crushed pineapple, ice, and sugar-water mixture. Mix thoroughly and serve in champagne glasses.

CHICHA DE FRUTAS

Fruit Beer

Yield: 1 gallon

1 small pineapple
1 gallon water
2 cups sugar
10 cloves
2 cinnamon sticks
2 apples, peeled and cored
2 quinces, peeled and seeds
removed (as many as you
can capture)
3 peaches, peeled and pitted

The state of Tabasco may be tiny, but its thirst is enormous. Every street corner has a straw-hatted vendor crooning the unique taste of his fresh fruit punches. The salesmen's rolling carts are heavy with huge glass jars, filled with jewel-toned juices.

This recipe is a combination of the fruits to be found in the heat of the tropical Gulf, and has a bit of a kick. Sometimes it is made with just pineapple and then it is called Tepache (see page 83)— delicious!

1. Wash the pineapple thoroughly and remove the rind. Crush the rind thoroughly and place it in a large pot with water, sugar, cloves, and cinnamon. Boil for 15 minutes, cool, and strain.
2. In the processor, purée the pineapple, apples, quinces, and peaches, and add to the pineapple-rind mixture. Allow to stand overnight.
3. Strain through a damp cloth napkin (or triple cheesecloth), pressing the fruit to extract all the flavor. Allow to stand at room temperature in an earthenware crock for 5 to 7 days, or until it ferments a little. It should taste "fizzy." Serve chilled.

"MUS" DE MANGO

Mango Mousse

Serves 6

1 small package peach gelatin
¾ cup boiling water
6 large ripe mangos or
   1 30-ounce can
1 cup sugar
juice of 3 limes
1 pint heavy cream, whipped
   stiff, sweetened to taste
4 egg whites, whipped until
   peaks form

Mangos grow all over tropical Mexico, and in the Gulf States whole hillsides are made green with their lush foliage and succulent fruit. Eating a fresh, juicy mango is an art . . . it also distinguishes the amateurs from the connoisseurs . . . the amateurs discard the pit, the gourmets suck on it until the last drop of nectar is enjoyed!

1. Dissolve the gelatin in boiling water. Set aside.
2. Slice the mango meat away from the pit or drain the canned mangoes,[1] and place in a blender or processor.
3. Purée the mango, sugar, lime juice, and dissolved gelatin.
4. Pour the mango mixture into a large bowl and stir in the whipped cream, blending well. Fold in egg whites.
5. Rinse a 2-quart mold with cold water and fill with the mango mixture. Chill in the refrigerator until set, at least 5 hours, and unmold onto a serving platter.

[1] Substitute juice for boiling water for a more concentrated flavor, or reserve for a fruit punch base.

FLAN DE NARANJA

Orange Custard

Serves 6

4 cups light cream
1 teaspoon vanilla
4 whole eggs and 2 yolks
¼ cup orange juice
2 tablespoons sugar
1 cup sugar
1 teaspoon orange zest
½ cup water
1 orange, peeled and sliced thin for garnish
chopped toasted almonds (optional garnish)

Flan is as Mexican as the taco, and one could write an entire cookbook about its variations. Because the Gulf is the vanilla belt where the bean-producing plantations nudge citrus groves, many cooks of the area combine the two ingredients in this classic Mexican sweet.

1. In a medium-sized saucepan, scald the cream. Continue to simmer until it reduces to about 3 cups. Add the vanilla and set aside.

2. In a large mixing bowl, beat together the eggs, yolks, orange juice, 2 tablespoons of sugar, and orange zest. Gradually pour in the hot cream mixture, stirring vigorously. Set aside.

3. Dissolve the cup of sugar in the water and heat this syrup in a heavy iron skillet until it is golden brown. Pour into 6 custard cups, twirling the cups quickly to coat the bottoms and sides. Let the caramel set.

4. Pour the custard into cups; set the cups in an oven pan of hot water. Bake at 325°F or until a knife inserted near the center comes out clean. Cool and unmold the cups on small dessert plates. Garnish with orange slices and chopped toasted almonds.

BUDÍN DE ARROZ DONA LALA

Rice Pudding

Serves 4

2 cups milk
½ cup rice, rinsed well
zest of 1 lemon
¾ cup sugar
3 tablespoons grated coconut
(fresh if possible)
2 tablespoons almonds,
blanched,[1] skinned, and
chopped fine
2 eggs + 1 yolk

Gazing out over the pier in Tlacotalpan, a friend and I enjoyed a delicious rice dessert which is the specialty of the Polada Doña Lala. Beacuse the chef was not available, and because we know the area abounds with umbrella-like almond trees and soaring coconut palms, here is the recipe I developed to commemorate that lazy afternoon. The recipe doubles well.

1. In a medium-sized saucepan, bring the milk to the boiling point and add the rice and lemon zest. Cook at a simmer for about 25 minutes or until the rice is tender, stirring occasionally to keep the mixture from sticking.

2. Add half the sugar, the coconut, and the almonds. Incorporate well.

3. Beat the eggs and yolk together and add to the above mixture a little at a time, stirring constantly.

4. Heat the oven to 350°F. In a small saucepan, caramelize the remaining sugar with a little water and pour into 4 individual baking or custard cups. Add the rice custard.

5. Set the dish in a pan of water and bake for about 1 hour, or until a knife inserted in the center comes out clean. Allow to cool and turn out onto a serving platter with a bowl of fresh strawberries in the center.

---

[1] To blanch the almonds, place the nuts in boiling water for several minutes and then pinch them between your thumb and forefinger to pull off the skins.

EL SURESTE

States of:

OAXACA, CHIAPAS

AND

CAMPECHE, YUCATÁN, QUINTANA ROO

EL SURESTE

When you mention the "Sureste" in Mexico, the inevitable follow-up question is, "what part?"—for the entire area is the Mexico of historical blood-letting and compelling paradoxes, but there is a subtle difference in the reasons for the ancient internecine strife of Oaxaca and Chiapas as compared to Campeche, Yucatán, and Quintana Roo.

The battles fought in Oaxaca were mostly between the Mixtec and Zapotec, both proud, bellicose, and disdainful of the other. Their temperaments and accomplishments should have complemented each other as intermarriage blurred the tribal lines, but the underlying animosity weakened them to the point where they first succumbed to the acquisitive Aztecs and then finally to the Spaniards in 1522.

Bearing the individualistic marks of its early dwellers, Oaxaca alone records 17 indigenous languages spoken, and many of the ancient but differing customs and crafts of these durable people are today alive and thriving. Each small village has its own kind of handwork, and even the embroidery styles and stitches vary from town to town.

Chiapas, even today, is a world apart. Topography also has lent a hand in its fractionalization. The terrain is breathtakingly beautiful but daunting to a burdened walker. In Mexico, no one travels empty-handed. In the case of the women, there is always a tortilla or bread basket perfectly balanced atop the neat, black braids. Indian villages in Chiapas may lie within a few kilometers of each other, yet the inhabitants cross paths only during market days.

The handsome Tzótziles, Tzéltales, Chamulans, and Zinacantecans are weavers extraordinaire. The pressures of civilization and its subsequent exploitation of simpler folk, are now being spotlighted in the headlines of the world. Members of the reclusive Lacandón tribe inhabit the hardwood forests, coming into the pueblos to buy or sell foodstuffs. Their distinctive, sloped-profiles have been immortalized by Mexican artists of the muralists' school. The indigenous food of this remote area is simple and basic, changing only with the offerings of the season.

● ● ● ●

Mayaland—Campeche, Yucatán, and Quintana Roo—held a generally cohesive view of the universe, but their rivalries were fueled by the need for arable land as their population increased. Families were so busy warring among themselves over land and each other's women, that when the Spaniards arrived, the glory that was the Mayan empire had largely tumbled, to be overgrown by the jungle. What little remains of that architectural splendor is mind-boggling, even in our high-tech times.

This thumbnail of history is supported by the cooking of these regions. Oaxaca has a rich inventory of specialties and is known as the "land of the seven *moles*." The refinements of Spanish cuisine have left their mark, tempered by the practical use of everything the earth has to offer. A sophisticated chicken with black *mole* (see page 264) may be accompanied by tacos of crisp, deep fried *chapulines* (grasshoppers), seasoned with salt and chili.

The Yucatán peninsula has a unique cuisine, marked by many ingredients harvested only in her boundaries. Known as the land of pheasant and deer, game abounds and is brought brilliantly to the table. The beckoning azure sea offers table treasures without par, and certain chilies (*Xtaciks, chile habañeros*) are grown only here. Produce is plentiful in the humid heat; a leafy green called *chaya* is much like spinach but not quite the same; Yucatecan red onions are world-famed; the limes are huge and sweeter than ours; and other tropical fruits outdo themselves in size and flavor.

THINGS TO SEE, DO, AND EAT

Oaxaca (City of): The Rufino Tamayo museum's treasures and drama set the mood for the entire experience of the area. Follow up with the splendid Museo Regional, where copies of Mexico's answer to Britain's crown jewels are on display. A good place to look at stelae and other sculpture taken from the sites of the ruins which you will soon see.

- **The Santo Domingo Church**: After the soaring paganism of Monte Albán, the contrast of the Santo Domingo Church is an experience not to be missed. The combination of white stucco and exuberant gold leaf reaches unimagined heights here, and the viewer wonders what the ghosts of this city might tell.

- **El Mercado Viejo** (the old market) on 20 Noviembre Street, **FONART** and **ARIPO** are the places to shop for weavings and embroideries. The latter two are government sponsored and receive new merchandise daily. If shopping for embroidered *huipiles* (loose blouses made from flour sacks, pronounced "we-peel-ays"), check out many of them before you buy one. Compare the difference in tightness and number of stitches in a design. They call the fine ones *de abuela* (grandmother's) because the older generation took more pride in its work and had more time. (I have a treasured, old San Antonino *huipil* that has 13 little dolls embroidered across the bosom. Today's San Antonino's will have five to seven in the same space, haphazardly sewn. The young fingers and needles have grown lazy!)

- **The ruins of Monte Albán** are a breathtaking experience—Mexico's answer to the great pyramids of Egypt. Try to go early in the morning, when the ghosts are still about, and imagine yourself a Zapotec ruler surveying his domain. I still dream about it. Make sure you go with a guide book.

- For an elegant dinner "a la Oaxaqueña" eat at **El Asador Vasco.** Though the name is Spanish, it is a fine place to order the different *moles* of the region.

- From the sublime to the ridiculous, but ridiculously delicious, have an early morning breakfast at **Abuelitas** (Grandma's) in the **Mercado de Abastos.**

- **Mi Casita** (Hidalgo Street) is the place to sate that adventuresome palate. It is probably the best of the city's regional restaurants.

Yagúl: A Zapotec stronghold with protective siting and interesting ruins and petroglyphs. White on white embroidered *huipiles* from the area are often sold in the parking lot.

Mitla: The surroundings disappoint but the friezes are still fresh and impressive. Coming back on the road, stop for lunch at **Cabo Kennedy.** Don't miss the *Mole Verde*.

San Bartolo Coyotepec: This is the home of the pre-Hispanic inspired black pottery made famous in our time by "Doña Rosa." Pots, shaped by hand without a potters' wheel, and small human figures, (often depicting a family group), are for sale for the appreciative. The clay is fired with a matte finish and then burnished by hand in floral and geometric designs.

Ocotlán: Has a wonderful Friday market, neither organized nor selective, but it has always been a favorite of mine. Look sharp, among the junk there are local craft treasures. Contemporary painter Rodolfo Morales works here on his acclaimed brilliant canvasses.

Arrazola: Look for the Jiménez and Morales families, wood sculptors whose poli-chromed works are collected worldwide. Imitators sell crude copies—be careful.

Teotitlán: Handmade tapestries and floor coverings. Charming, woven, rough copies of famous modern paintings. Bargain by all means . . . it's expected.

Puerto Escondido: Dusty and surfer-infested, the town is a resort waiting to happen. Until then, the Santa Fé and Posada Real Hotels have private beaches and are quite lovely. Two good restaurants are **La Perla Flamante** and the "beach bum" favorite of mine, **Lolis**.

Puerto Angel: Avoid it like the plague!

Huatulco: Accessible now only by air or second-class bus, this is a breathtaking paradise for the beach lover—about to be completely ruined by resort development. The hammers and radios of workman have already begun their erosion in town. There is a first-class Sheraton in Santa Cruz Huatulco, but much better for unspoiled beauty is the Club Med across the bay.

Juchitán: Worth mentioning as a gourmand tourist destination, just to try their *Tamales etEbinguis*. These are made of corn masa which has the added crunch of small bits of pork cracklings (*chicharrón*) filled with little shrimp, toasted sunflower seeds, green chile, and annato flavoring, steamed in a clay pot sunk in an earthen pit. Divine, but it's a long, dusty trip for a munchie!

CHIAPAS

Palenque: The ruins are worth the heart-stopping aerial puddle jump, but I for one prefer to drive from Villa Hermosa. Wherever you stay, always empty your shoes before putting them on. Remember, this is jungle, and creepy crawlers like to hide in dark, unlikely places.

San Cristóbal de las Casas: This is another world. Conflict, as it has been novelized in B. Traven's writings, has ever been the architect here, but its fascination for the visitor is everlasting. There's so much to see!

On the steps leading to the Dominican-built **Santo Domingo Church**, men from San Juán Chamula (many converted to Protestantism and pariahs in their own villages), hold discourse at small extemporaneous altars lining the entry stairs. Incense burns inside and outside, and packets of curative potions are sold or bartered.

Schedule a visit to **Na Bolom**, the home/museum/gallery of Trudy Blom, long a champion of the local Lacandón indians.

The butterfly museum, **Museo Zul-Pepen** is another must.

The market here is a daily one and is where the individualistic embroidery of the women of the outlying villages is sold. The men of the region wear the most brilliant and richly embroidered costumes, as well as marvelous straw hats with ribbons and beads dangling from them.

The **Diego de Mazariegos** has a fine restaurant, but it is a stronghold for rude French tourists. A good restaurant for the real feel of San Cristobal is **El Conquistador**; another, although "Frenchified," is **El Teatro**. (No, I am not a Francophobe, I just prefer *my* Mexico to be Mexican!)

CAMPECHE

If you're into hats, then this is the stop from Villa Hermosa to Mérida. The local markets and boutiques sell the Mexican version of *jipijapa*, Panamanian-style hats which are made in the pueblito of Becal. Several years ago I bought them in eight colors, and because they are indestructible, there's no reason to go back to the genteely tacky city.

YUCATÁN

An otherworldly place to visit, but only in the cool months, that is from November to February. Otherwise heat, humidity, and mosquitos can make the region a hell!

During the magical winter months however, there is no place on earth more friendly or fascinating. Base in Mérida and head for the tourist office, ask a million questions, read everything they offer (in several languages), and don't settle simply for Chichen-Itzá.

Warning here: Public transportation is iffy—unless you are on a strict budget, splurge here for a car and guide or make arrangements for tours. Uxmal and Chichén-Itzá of course, but other sites to consider are: Kabáh, Sayil, Xlapak, and Labná.

If you're a bit of a closet spelunker, the Yucatán is cross hatched with caves which the Mayan considered entrances to the subterranean world of the gods. The most trafficked are the Caves at Loltún and Balankanche, but any good guide can turn up a noncommercialized one or two, as well as his own *cenote* (sacred whirlpool or bathing place).

Mérida: Buy embroidered *huipiles* (tunics fashioned from bleached flour sacks). Splurge on one of the hand-embroidered ones, they're expensive, but are becoming collector's items); hammocks, Becal hats (if you didn't get to Campeche), baskets, weavings, and Guayabera shirts for men.

Mérida Hotels: By all means try to get reservations at the top of the line, the **Casa de Balam** for elegance and charm. *Note*: Most of the major archeologic sites have their own hotels. Book well in advance because rooms are numbered. Again, consult a good guidebook or the tourist office in Mérida.

Restaurants: For many, the very best food in Mexico with the fiery, local Habañero chilies usually served on the side. The fine seafood of the surrounding waters is done best justice at **Muelle 8**. The Mérida branch of the family-style **Los Almendros** (mentioned elsewhere in these pages) serves the delicious specialties of the region (see recipe pages); the dining room at the **Gran Hotel** is an experience, and don't miss breakfast at the **Express**.

QUINTANA ROO

Cancún: A place to avoid, unless you are 17 and looking for rip-off priced thrills (see box page 14). If you are bound and determined to get to the sea, or have won a sales incentive tour, head out to Kilometer 13 and the **Paraíso Radisson**, pleasant luxury, but less glitz—more of the real feel of Mexico and a much more reasonable tab at the end of your stay.

Shopping: Don't! Check out the window displays in the air conditioned malls and then buy what you covet somewhere else in the Republic . . . Talk about gouging!

BEACHES

- Exclusive **Playa Akumal** which means Place of the Turtles.

- **Playa Chemuyil**, once known as the "most beautiful beach in the world," is now people polluted and a disappointment.

- **Playa Xcacal** (shkah-cahl), is a magical place with thatched palapas sheltering hammocks, few tourists, and even a shipwreck for drama.

- **Playas Tulum.** After perusing the ruins (often spoiled by cola cans), head down the beach to the sea turtle preserve, Sian Ka'an. During nesting season the area may be closed, so check with someone before you trek.

Cozumel: An expensive place for serious snorkeling and scuba diving. Make sure you have a drink or a meal at the **Stouffer Presidente. La Misión** caters to a sedate senior crowd who appreciate the wonderful food.

Chetumal: You've almost run out of Mexico, and unless you tolerate heat well, coming this far is really not worth it. Accommodations and food are underwhelming.

OAXACA

AND

CHIAPAS

SOPA DE PAN

Bread Soup

Serves 6

6 cups chicken stock
2 carrots, peeled and coarsely
   chopped
1 2-inch stick cinnamon
1 sprig thyme
1 sprig marjoram
1/2 teaspoon freshly ground
   pepper
1/4 cup dry white wine
salt, to taste
3 cups cubed white bread
   (baguette or hard roll),
   toasted
2 tablespoons butter or
   margarine
2 tablespoons oil
1 large onion, sliced
3 cloves garlic
1 1/2 pounds tomatoes, peeled and thickly sliced
1/4 cup raisins
3 hard-cooked eggs
ground cinnamon
1/2 cup crumbled *queso añejo* (or Feta cheese)

1. Place the chicken stock, carrots, cinnamon, thyme, marjoram, pepper, and wine in a large saucepan. Bring to a boil, cover, and cook over medium heat for 10 minutes, or until the carrots are tender. Add salt to taste. Discard the cinnamon, thyme, and marjoram, and set the stock aside.
2. Heat the butter in a large skillet. Add half the bread cubes and fry for a few minutes or until they are golden brown. Transfer to a plate covered with absorbent paper. Repeat the procedure with the rest of the bread cubes. Set aside.

Fiercely beautiful Chiapas is a poor state. Still uncharted are many of its jungles or craggy reaches, torn by tribalism, and fomented by the encroachment of an exploitive bureaucracy.

After a day of pondering the sharp contrast of opulent churches and the dignified poverty obvious in the markets and side streets, it's time for the appreciation of a bowl of something steamy. This is a peasant soup, hearty and complex as are the handsome, skirted inhabitants whose land this is.

3. Heat the oil in the same skillet, add the onion and garlic, and sauté for 3 minutes. Add the tomatoes and raisins and cook over medium heat, stirring constantly, for 10 minutes. Set aside.

4. Fifteen minutes before serving, preheat the oven to 425°F. Bring the reserved chicken stock to a simmer. Divide the bread cubes, stewed tomatoes, and raisins among 6 ovenproof bowls, and add the hot chicken stock. Garnish with 2 slices of egg and a dash of cinnamon. Bake until the soup starts to boil. Serve hot, sprinkled with the *queso añejo*.

MOLE NEGRO DE OAXACA

In line with my strong feelings about simplifying regional Mexican dishes, I'm going to rhapsodize about this glorious dish, but not give a recipe for it. To quote Zarela Martínez (*Food From My Heart*, MacMillan):

> *You may think it (the recipe) couldn't possibly be worth the trouble when you look at the long list of ingredients and procedures, but I assure you the end result is always rewarding.*

I feel only a superb restaurateur, as is Martínez, who has a culinary staff for some of the kitchen busy work, would attempt the dish—I slogged through it in Mexico with Sabina at my side, but my Boston kitchen has no auxiliary hands.

In addition, another cooking idol of mine, Rick Bayless (*Authentic Mexican*, William Morrow), substitutes the Mole from Puebla, because the black *chilhuacle negros*, vital to the authentic flavor and perfume of this dish, are not available in the United States.

I'm going to list the contents and urge you to look for and order anything on a Oaxacan menu which contains *Mole Negro*. Also particularly delicious and available everywhere in Mexico, are the *Tamales Estilo Oaxaqueño*, filled with shredded pork or chicken, lavished with the *mole*, and then wrapped in a neat, flat square of banana leaves.

Partial list of ingredients:

2 kinds of dried chilies	cloves
plantain	cinnamon
shortening	oregano
sesame seeds	dry sherry
peppercorns	onion
3 kinds of nuts, walnuts,	fresh tomatoes
almonds, peanuts	sweet roll
Mexican bitter chocolate	dried fruits
chicken broth	tomatillos

LENTEJAS CON FRUTA

Lentils with Fruit

Serves 6

Oaxaca simply bursts with creativity—perhaps the view from the summits of Monte Albán's temples inspired the Zapotecan rulers to demand special treatment from the royal cooks. This meal-in-a-dish is my simplified, lower fat variation of a recipe from Mexico the Beautiful Cookbook.

2 cups dried lentils
8 cups chicken broth
½ pound spicy sausage, casings removed and chopped into pieces
1 cup chopped onion
3 cloves garlic, minced
3 slices fresh pineapple, chopped (or canned chunks)
1 plantain or large, firm banana, peeled, and sliced
1 teaspoon salt
½ teaspoon freshly ground pepper
2 tablespoons vegetable oil
2½ pound rounds of smoked ham (see note)
6 scallions, chopped

1. Rinse the lentils and add to a large saucepan. Cover with broth and bring to a boil. Lower the heat and simmer, covered, for 45 minutes. Drain, and reserving the cooking liquid.
2. In another large saucepan, sauté the sausage, covered, for 5 minutes. Drain off the excess fat. Add the onion and garlic and sauté for 3 more minutes. Add the lentils, pineapple, plantain, salt, and pepper, and cook, covered, over low heat, for 10 minutes, adding broth if the mixture becomes too dry.
3. Stir in 2 cups of the reserved liquid, cover, and simmer for 30 additional minutes.
4. While the lentil mixture is cooking, heat the oil in a skillet. Cut the ham rounds into thirds and sauté for 2–3 minutes on each side. Transfer to the pan with the lentils and cook, covered, for 5 minutes. Serve topped with the chopped scallions.

Note: Pork butt or smoked pork chops may be used. Because the chops are sometimes hard to find, and both cuts can be very salty, I rely on the ham.

ROLLOS DE PAVO EN SALSA DE CACAHUATE

Turkey Rolls in Peanut Sauce

Serves 6

Mitla's friezes are a wonder, but the ghosts that frequent ruins are in hiding during the day, frightened perhaps by the hawking of the market vendors who disturb the antiquity of the scene. Close your eyes to the noise and commerce and work up an appetite for this specialty of nearby Oaxaca City.

12 turkey cutlets, pounded thin
freshly ground black pepper
12 thin slices boiled ham
    (honey cured is extra good)
3 tablespoons of vegetable oil
3 tablespoons of minced onion
¼ teaspoon ground cinnamon
4 tablespoons of thick tomato purée
4 tablespoons of smooth peanut butter
2 canned chipotle chilies, seeds removed and mashed
    (use some of the juice)
¾ cup of chicken broth
vegetable shortening for frying
½ cup unsalted, roasted peanuts, slightly crushed

1. Sprinkle the cutlets lightly with pepper and place a slice of ham on each cutlet.
2. In a medium-sized skillet, heat the oil and sauté the onion, until transparent. Add the cinnamon, tomato purée, peanut butter, and mashed chilies. Blend well into a smooth paste.
3. Spread a dollop of the paste over each slice of ham, roll the turkey/ham/filling into a fat cigar shape, and secure with a string or a toothpick. Thin the rest of the paste to a gravy consistency with the chicken broth. Keep at a simmer, adding broth if necessary.
4. In a large skillet, heat the shortening and fry the turkey rolls until light golden brown. Remove to a heated serving platter. Serve sprinkled with crushed, roasted peanuts with any extra sauce on the side.

MANCHAMANTELES

"Tablecloth Stainer"

Serves 6

The origins of this dish are said to be Oaxacan, but it is found on Comidas Corridas' daily, in every pueblito in Mexico. The combination of fruit and meat is a common one in the warmer portions of the country, perhaps because the fruit is available for the reaching!

5 ancho chiles, seeds and
    membrane removed
1 teaspoon cinnamon
3 whole cloves
4 black peppercorns
½ cup almonds, blanched
½ teaspoon each dried oregano and thyme
4 tablespoons vegetable oil
3 large ripe tomatoes, peeled and chopped
1 pound lean, boneless pork shoulder, cut into pieces
1 frying chicken, cut into serving pieces
1½–2 cups water
1 teaspoon salt
1 small sprig parsley
1 sweet potato, peeled and cubed
1 tablespoon butter or margarine
2 slices pineapple, cubed
2 cups sliced plantain or large firm banana
1 small jícama, peeled and cut into 1¼-inch cubes

1. Roast the chiles on a griddle or in a iron skillet, turning often so that they blister all over. Soak in hot water to cover for 20 minutes. Drain.

2. In a heavy skillet, toast the cinnamon, cloves, peppercorns, almonds, oregano, and thyme, shaking the pan almost continuously. Transfer to a blender, add the chiles, and purée.

3. Heat 1 tablespoon of the oil in a large saucepan. Add the spiced chile purée, and bring to a bubble, stirring constantly, for 5 minutes. Do not wash the blender jar.

---

[1] The daily, prix fixe menu—throughout Mexico, it is the buy of the land. For just a few pesos, you'll be offered a soup (dry or wet), a main course, beans, rice, and hot tortillas. The usual cost is between 80 cents and a dollar.

4. In the blender jar, purée the tomatoes. Add to the chile purée, lower the heat, and cook for 5 minutes, stirring constantly. Set aside.

5. In a large, heavy skillet, heat the remaining oil, add the pork and chicken pieces, and sauté until lightly browned. Add the water, salt, and parsley. When the water comes to a boil, lower the heat and cook, covered, for 10 minutes. Add the chile sauce and continue cooking for 10 minutes. Add the sweet potato and cook for an additional 10 minutes.

6. Melt the butter in a small skillet, sauté the pineapple, plantain, and jícama until lightly browned. Add to the pork, adjust the seasonings, and cook, covered, over low heat for 15 minutes, or until the pork is tender and the chicken cooked. Serve in a covered casserole or tureen with white rice and hot tortillas.

THE ORIGINAL
DEATH BY
CHOCOLATE

To the Aztecs in Mexico's high, central plateaus goes the credit for the discovery of the cocoa bean in the early 1500s.

Originally, they ground the almond-shaped seed with corn, sweetened it with honey, spices, and a touch of chili, then thinned it with water. Once the mixture was made, a decoratively-carved, wooden beater was rolled rapidly between the palms and a high foam was created—the foam was then separated from the heavier mass and set aside. After various repetitions of the process, the collected foam only was consumed.

The drink was then enjoyed at room temperature, but the cold mountain winters of Tenochtitlán brought the drink to the braziers and it became an all-season delight.

One of the most bewitching stories about Latin-American chocolate addiction is the following from *Historia de La Comida en Mexico* (see bibliography).

In 1625, a startling crime shocked the southern Mexican region of Chiapas . . . the murder of Bishop Bernardino Salazar y Frías. The motive for the killing was the Holy man's edict that the chocolate break during mass be abolished!

The ladies of the time broke the monotony of the interminable daily masses (over which long-winded Father

Salazar officiated) with extravagant parades of liveried servants carrying linen-swathed, small tables. Upon the tables, served in European china cups, and silver dishes and plates, were placed the omnipresent, steaming chocolate and a variety of sweet breads and cookies.

Now, imagine the clatter and crunch of this daily spectacle! The poor bishop was so distracted by this practice, which also occasioned much feminine chatter and subsequent ignorance of the seriousness of the mass, that the exasperated priest one day forbade the practice.

The ladies countered by refusing to attend mass.

Chapter two in the saga: The beleagured bishop pronounced *ipso facto* group excommunication of the frivolous and disobedient ladies.

The city was in an uproar, and despite the well-intentioned intervention of the local government and other clergy, the impasse continued. Chocolate—no mass—mass—no chocolate.

Next, the ladies started an ingenious, whispering campaign against the man of God, and so aroused their spouses, that the distaff dissenters managed to fire the town's manhood into laying siege to the cathedral. There were wounded, but still no solution.

The ladies now took direct action. They began to have delivered to the bishop (three or four times daily), exquisitely presented repasts of chocolate and sweets, accompanied by cajoling notes asking for forgiveness. Within a week, the Bishop fell ill and died, his disagreement with the "chocolate break" forever stilled by his arsenic-laced enjoyment of the controversial drink.

The ladies flicked their fans and blew on their chocolate cups during the entire funeral.

If there's a moral, it must be, "Don't cross a chocoholic." Historically, they can be **mean!**

PIPIÁN VERDE

Pumpkin Seed Sauce

Serves 8

The original of this much-simplified version is a regional glory of the state of Oaxaca, the home of the Zapotec and Mixtec Indian tribes. There it simmers away for hours, perfuming the archeological sites of Monte Albán and Mitla. Versions of this savory sauce may be found all through the Republic, masquerading under a variety of names: Salsa Verde de Pepita, Adobo Verde, Mole Verde, and others.

3 canned or 2 fresh Jalapeño
   chiles
1/3 cup sesame or vegetable oil
1 large onion quartered
3 garlic cloves, peeled
3 green peppers, peeled,
   and seeded
large bunch of fresh coriander/
   cilantro
6 spinach or outer romaine
   leaves
2 pounds tomatillos, husked and chopped
1 cup pumpkin seeds (peeled and toasted)
1/3 cup honey
2 tablespoons peanut butter
1/4 teaspoon ground cumin
1/4 teaspoon allspice
1 ounce anisette liqueur (optional)

1. Rinse and open the Jalapeños under cold water, handling carefully. Discard the seeds and the white veins.
2. Heat the oil in a large skillet. Add the Jalapeños, onion, garlic, and green peppers. Sauté together lightly.
3. Remove the coriander/cilantro leaves from the stems, wash them along with the spinach (or romaine) leaves. Shake dry in a towel or spinner and add to the skillet along with the tomatillos and the pumpkin seeds. Continue to sauté until the mixture is "mushy," stirring constantly with a wooden spoon.
4. Remove from the flame and purée the mixture in a blender or food processor until smooth—it will be grainy.
5. Add honey, peanut butter, cumin, and allspice. Purée a few seconds longer and remove to a double boiler to keep warm until serving time. Just before serving you may add the anisette, if desired.

Note: This is traditionally served over roast pork, chicken, turkey, or any wild fowl. White rice is the usual accompaniment, and, of course, fresh, piping hot tortillas. I serve this with a light red wine like Pinot Noir.

ENSALADA DE RÁBANOS

Radish Salad

Serves 6

3 cups radishes, scrubbed and
   chopped
½ cup white vinegar
2 teaspoons salt
1 cup of water
⅓ cup olive oil
3 tablespoons wine vinegar
4 good twists of freshly ground
   black pepper
1 large Jalapeño pepper, seeded,
   deveined, and julienned
4 radish roses

In December, Oaxaca celebrates a unique annual festival honoring their radish crop. The genus of cruciferae, which is cultivated extensively in the area, grow extra large and while growing, twist and turn in the earth into fanciful shapes. During the pre-Christmas holidays competitions are held for the largest, most grotesque, funniest, etc. entries. It's said that the campesinos often pay the local curanderos (folk doctors), for spells to make their radishes unique . . . quién sabe?

1. Soak the radishes in a solution of vinegar, salt, and water for several hours (this will make them crisp and remove some of the bite!). Drain.
2. In a small bowl, whisk together the oil, vinegar, and pepper.
3. Dress the radishes with the vinaigrette, toss well, and garnish with strips of Jalapeño and whole radish roses.

DULCE DE GARBANZO Y PIÑA OAXAQUEÑA

Chickpea and Pineapple Dessert

Serves 6

1 cup cooked Spanish
   chickpeas, well drained
½ cup molasses or dark Karo
   syrup
1 cup water
½ cup pineapple juice
1 cup crushed pineapple
sweet cream

1. In a 2-quart saucepan, mix the molasses or Karo with water and pineapple juice. Bring to a boil.
2. Mash the chickpeas and blend with the pineapple. Add to the boiling liquid and simmer, stirring constantly, until the pudding thickens.
3. Spoon into bowls and serve warm, topped with sweet cream.

Note: This is also delicious topped with a scoop of vanilla ice cream.

The beautiful city of Oaxaca seems to stand firm against the ravages of tourism. Each time I return, I expect vast changes—but the moon-faced locals are courteous, the city is cleaner and quieter than I remember it (the "Hondas from hell motorbikes," have found another venue), and the Zócalo again has chatting elders, vendors of things delicious and exotic, and all in all, the feeling that time has stood still.

For all of its intense indigenous feeling,[1] the Spanish influence is strong here, particularly in the architecture. The use of chickpeas in this simple, local dessert is also indicative of that influence.

---

[1] There are seventeen different ethnic groups in the state of Oaxaca, each with its own language and customs.

DULCE DE PAPAYA AMAMEYADA

Baked Red Papaya Trifle

Serves 6

The glorious fruits of the tropics inspire most desserts, and this specialty of Oaxaca, blends several cultures to emphasize the unique flavor of the red papaya of the region. The rosy fruit is not only sweeter, but it has less of the off-putting aroma of its yellow cousin.

1 cup water
¾ cup sugar
½ cup sweet sherry
2 pounds of fresh red papaya
(can substitute 2 small
Hawaiian papayas)
3 cups milk
20 ladyfingers
30 whole almonds, skinned and toasted

1. In a small saucepan, heat the water and sugar together, stirring, until it reaches a syrup consistency. Remove from the heat and add the wine, allowing the liquid to cool.

2. Peel and purée the papaya (in a food processor or Mouli-type grater) and place the pulp in a large saucepan with half of the wine syrup and the milk. On low heat, allow the mixture to cook until it reaches an applesauce-like consistency.

3. Grease an ovenware casserole dish and lay down a layer of ladyfingers. Top with the fruit purée and repeat with another layer of ladyfingers. Soak the ladyfingers with the remaining wine syrup and bake for 30–40 minutes in a 350°F oven until nicely browned. Decorate with daisies formed from the almonds.

AGUA DE HORCHATA

Ground Rice Drink

Serves 6–8

2 cups long-grain white rice
2 quarts (8 cups) water
2 4-inch cinnamon sticks or
    1 teaspoon ground
1 cup almonds, blanched
2 cups milk
1 cup sugar, or to taste

The Southeast can become pretty steamy in the summer, and it's hard to think of any beverage more cooling than horchata. In Oaxaca and the Yucatán it is made with ground rice, and in other parts of the country, melon seeds are used.

1. Grind the rice fine in a minichopper or blender. In a large bowl, soak the ground rice in 3 cups of hot water for at least 4 hours. Drain the rice and discard the water.

2. Pulverize the cinnamon sticks and almonds and add the ground rice. Continue processing until no longer grainy. Add the milk and 4 cups of water. Cover and refrigerate overnight in a mixing bowl.

3. Strain the mixture through double cheese cloth into a pitcher and dilute with 4 cups of cold water. Add sugar to taste.

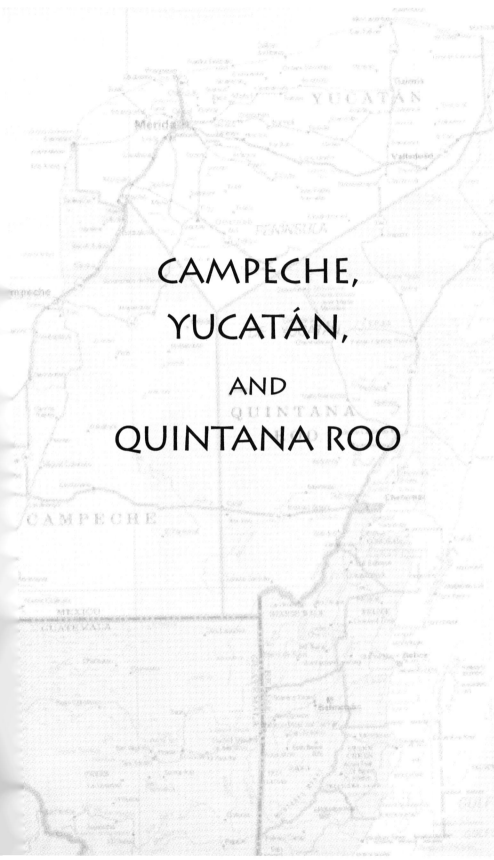

CAMPECHE,
YUCATÁN,
AND
QUINTANA ROO

SOPA DE LIMA

Yucatecan Lime Soup

Serves 6

Valladolid is a charming, little, colonial town—perfect for a "break-up-the-trip to Chichen-Itzá"—overnight. The Mesón del Marqués has a flower-laden courtyard where the visitor can enjoy sumptuous breakfasts al fresco, or a steaming bowl of this Mayan specialty.

2 tablespoons vegetable oil
3 cloves garlic, minced
1 medium-sized onion, chopped
6 cups chicken broth
1 8-ounce can plum tomatoes
3 tablespoons chopped fresh coriander/cilantro
1 teaspoon Tabasco or other hot sauce
juice of 1 lime (a lemon is acceptable but not as flavorful)
1 cup cooked, white meat chicken, shredded
salt and pepper, to taste
½ bag of unsalted tortilla "chips," broken in half
1 cup white cheese (like Feta or goat cheese), crumbled
6 slices of lime for garnish

1. In a heavy soup pot, heat the oil and sauté the garlic and onion until transparent. Add the chicken broth, tomatoes, coriander/cilantro, and Tabasco, and simmer for 30 minutes, covered.
2. Add the lime juice and chicken and simmer long enough to heat the chicken. Season to taste with salt and pepper.
3. Divide into 6 bowls, top with tortilla chips and cheese, and garnish with a lime slice. Serve very hot.

Note: If you want a one-dish meal, add white rice and a more generous portion of chicken per serving.

SOPA DE GARBANZOS CAMPECHANA

Chickpea Soup, Campeche-style

Serves 6

2 tablespoons olive oil
1 large onion, chopped
1 clove garlic
2 cups cooked chickpeas
  (1 16-ounce can)
2 tablespoons flour
¼ teaspoon salt
4 cups chicken stock
2 sprigs *epazote* (see page 26)
  or
  1 teaspoon dried
¼ teaspoon chili powder
1 tablespoon butter

1. Heat the oil in a soup pot with a cover. Sauté the onion and garlic until golden brown. Drain the chickpeas, reserving the liquid, and sauté 2 or 3 minutes.
2. Add the chickpea liquid and simmer slowly, 5 minutes.
3. Whisk the flour into 2 tablespoons of water. Add the salt, stock, *epazote*, and chili powder and simmer for 5 minutes. Just before serving, add the butter, and serve at once.

Jaina (high-na) is a tiny island, a scant hundred feet off the coast of Campeche. It's name, translated from the ancient Maya means "house on the water," and it is the site of some of the most exquisite pre-Columbian pottery ever unearthed.

Jaina sculptures (600–900 A.D.) might be called poetry in pottery. The pieces have an unequalled delicacy of feature and posture. Their models were the classic, stocky Mayans with their pitched foreheads and prominent noses, but the polychroming is more subtle than that of other cultures. Most striking is the wealth of subject and detail guiding us back in time to their everyday pursuits: hunting, fishing, weaving, parenting, and making love. You wonder if the artisans had any idea of the immortality their crafts have afforded.

Chickpeas may have come to the island via the Spanish missionaries who were the first to appreciate, but also lay to plunder, the ancient genius of the gentle fisherfolk of Jaina.

SOPA DE PESCADO CAMPECHANA

Fish Soup, Campeche-style

Serves 6–8

½ pound skate, cusk, pout
(any inexpensive fish
will do)
3 fish heads
3 cups water
4 cloves garlic
1 teaspoon marjoram
2 sprigs mint
2 scallions, chopped, with most
of the green tops
1 medium-sized onion,
chopped
1 egg yolk
¼ teaspoon pepper
¼ teaspoon nutmeg
1 tablespoon vegetable
shortening
½ sweet pepper, chopped
4 medium-sized tomatoes,
peeled and chopped
1 tablespoon lime juice
salt, to taste
1 teaspoon flour
4 slices toast, cut in small squares

Another charming custom of the Gulf and Sureste are the décimos. The name is a play on words—decimos, without the accent, means—"we say," and with the accent means "tens." With or without the little mark it refers to ten line poems about someone at the table, which are made up spontaneously by jovial members of a group at a gathering. The trick is to be amusing (ribaldry encouraged) and quick, because if you delay too long, you are forced to chug-a-lug your drink.

This recipe from the region might be called Mexican "gefilte fish." The combination with mint is not unusual in the area. Mint is also used to flavor chicken soup.

1. In a large pot, simmer the fish and fish heads, water, 2 cloves of garlic, marjoram, mint, and scallions for about 20 minutes or until the fish flakes.

2. Remove the fish from the broth, shred the edible meat, and mix with one-half of the onion, 2 sprigs of parsley, the egg yolk, pepper, and nutmeg. Shape the mixture into small balls. Discard the heads and bones.

3. In a large skillet, heat the shortening, and sauté other half of the chopped onion, the remaining garlic cloves, and the chopped sweet pepper. Add the rest of the parsley and the tomatoes and allow to cook for a minute or 2. Add the fish broth and balls, lime juice, and salt to taste. Sauté all together for 5 minutes.

4. Remove the fish balls to a heated serving vessel and keep warm. In a small bowl, blend the flour with one-quarter cup of water. Add a little at a time to the soup. Allow the soup to simmer, stirring gently, for 10 minutes. Pour over the fish balls and serve tiny squares of toast on the side or as a garnish.

NUTRITIVE
AND
EXPLOSIVE

Boiled, Fried, and Refried—Beautiful Beans

Why are the various stars of the legume family denigrated in many sophisticated cultures? It's a kind of reflex *esnobismo*, as they say in the Hispanic "barrios" all over the world—they are usually not expensive, God Bless 'em!

Tortillas, rice, and beans—but above all **beans**—are the three staples of the Mexican diet, providing the perfectly balanced diet, which although not generally considered gourmet fare, has sustained the hardy cinnamon-skinned "Mexicanos" for a thousand years.

Subject to change and trends, our new passion for healthy nutrition and the benefits to be accrued, are making us reevaluate past food prejudices. As a bonus, we are also discovering that some of these foods are also tantalizingly delicious. Are you ready to accept the Mexican maxim, that no meal, no matter how many pesos you own, is complete and "proper" without *refritos* or *de olla*.

As with chilies, the variety of beans grown and available is dizzying. Black beans (smaller than the ones to which we're accustomed); candy-striped *flor de mayo*, sepia toned *bayos*; brilliant gold *canarios*; and my favorite, the delicate, pinkish *pintos*.

When ordering beans in a restaurant you may be surprised with an elongated platter carrying a *"brazo"* (arm) of "refrieds," smothered with grated cheese and topped with a hackle of fried tortilla triangles. The "arms" may all look alike, but what an exquisite complexity of flavor and seasoning they are capable of . . . each of the leguminous cousins has its own perfume and flavor. I for one, would prefer to attend "bean tastings" to many of the long-winded oenophilic sessions where "color, body, and nose" are preliminaries to an often pretentious ceremony, and one always comes away hungry.

De Olla, means "from the pot," simple enough even for those of us who repeatedly failed secondary school Spanish 101. New Englanders have long known that nothing, but nothing makes beans taste better than subjecting them to long hours of warm confinement in a clay bean pot. The addition of a wedge of onion and a chunk of lard or fatback, hurts the flavor not at all. The Mexican departure from venerable Yankee recipes (and we all know which procedure predates whose!—Moctezuma's bones have moldered longer than John Alden's!), is the inclusion of more liquid so that the finished Latin American version is more "soupy" and generally eaten with a spoon directly from individual pots.

The *refritos* each cook prepares daily, are a marvelous mystery package waiting to be opened and enjoyed. Some have bits of *chorizo* (spicy sausage) or finely diced potatoes. Others reveal fried onions and the favorite chili of the region or household. A lesser known favorite of some of the Northern Mexican states is made with cream cheese and milk, and these indeed are the "beans that taste memories are made of ". . . wakening you at midnight with an akin to pregnancy craving.

Otra tortilla por favor, and I'll take my beans any way!

SOPA DE TORTUGA, ESTILO CAMPECHE

Turtle Soup, Campeche-style

Serves 4

2 tablespoons olive oil
3 medium-sized onions
3 medium-sized tomatoes, peeled
1 sweet pepper
3 cloves garlic, minced
1 clove
¼ teaspoon cinnamon
¼ teaspoon marjoram
⅛ teaspoon cumin
½ teaspoon pepper
½ teaspoon salt
½ pound turtle meat, chopped (can be purchased in cans)
½ cup stuffed olives, chopped
1 teaspoon capers, chopped
2 cups clam juice
1 tablespoon vinegar (any variety)
1 teaspoon flour
2 tablespoons white wine
3 sprigs parsley, finely chopped
3 slices toast

Although sea turtles are on the endangered species list, their meat remains a favorite eating delicacy in coastal areas. Land turtles and terrapins are also edible, but less delicate in flavor. Here is the Mexican version of the European soup.

This recipe falls into the category of sopa secas, dry soups, in that it is served over toast a la king-style. To convert to a soup, add four cups of chicken broth.

1. Heat the oil in a medium-sized stock pot. Chop the onions, tomatoes, sweet pepper, and garlic very fine, and sauté until limp.
2. Add the spices, salt, turtle meat, olives, capers, clam juice, and vinegar. Bring the mixture to the boiling point.
3. Whisk the flour into the wine and add, while stirring, to the hot mixture. Add the parsley. Stew for 5 minutes. Serve on small squares of toast.

ESCABECHE DE CEBOLLA CHIXULUB

. . . .

Pickled Red Onion Relish

Yield: 2 cups

4 tablespoons olive oil
3 medium-sized red onions,
  sliced thin
4 cloves garlic, peeled
½ teaspoon oregano
½ teaspoon dried thyme, or
  1 large sprig fresh
3 whole cloves
½ teaspoon black peppercorns
⅓ cup wine vinegar

1. In a large skillet, heat the oil and quickly sauté the onion and garlic.

2. Stir in the oregano, thyme, cloves, peppercorns, vinegar, and just enough water to cover. Simmer for about 3 minutes. Remove to a glass dish with a cover. Allow the flavors to meld for several hours.

Note: Will keep for several weeks in the refrigerator or indefinitely in the freezer.

The fishing village of Chixulub is a marvelous place to enjoy the wriggly catch of the day. Sitting on the tables of "Los Tiburones" (The Sharks) a local hangout, you'll find a glass bowl of this Yucatecan treat, to add spice to your fresh grilled skate wings, shark, or snapper.

Warning: When you make it, double the recipe. It goes well with everything from Pibil and Poc Choc to cream cheese sandwiches and it's definitely an addictive accompaniment.

Another tip: If you like your onions strong, choose them round or elongated; for milder flavors, buy the flattish ones.

CAMARONES A LA YUCATECA

Chilled Shrimp with Yucatecan Lime dressing

Serves 4

The crystalline waters which meet at the apex of the Bay of Campeche and the Mexican Caribbean abound with a particularly succulent variety of small shrimp. I find that to approximate their wonderful, briny flavor it is better to use our medium-large variety.

For the shrimp:
1 lime, halved
1 teaspoon pickling spices, very coarsely ground
2 pounds medium-large shrimp (28–32 to the pound), left in their shells

For completing the dish:
1/2 small red onion, cut into 1/4-inch dice
2 ripe, plum tomatoes, cored and cut into 1/4-inch dice
1 1/2 tablespoons finely chopped fresh coriander/cilantro
3–4 tablespoons freshly squeezed lime juice (lemon may be substituted)
5 tablespoons virgin olive oil
1/2 teaspoon oregano, dried
1/4 teaspoon chili powder (optional)
1/2 teaspoon salt
2 or 3 leaves romaine or leaf lettuce, for garnish
sprigs of coriander/cilantro or radish roses, for garnish

1. Squeeze the juice from the 2 lime halves into a medium-sized saucepan, then add the 2 squeezed rinds, the pickling spices, and 1 quart of water. Cover and simmer over medium-low heat for 10 minutes.
2. Raise the heat to high, add the shrimp, replace the cover, and let the liquid return to a full boil. Immediately remove the pan from the heat, hold the lid slightly askew, and strain off all the liquid. Replace the cover tightly, set aside for 12 minutes, then rinse the shrimp under cold water to stop the cooking.

3. Peel the shrimp, then devein them by running a knife down the back to expose the dark intestinal track and scraping it out. Place the shrimp in a large glass bowl.

4. Add the red onion, tomatoes, and coriander/cilantro to the shrimp. In a small bowl, combine the lime juice, oil, oregano, chili powder, and salt. Toss with the shrimp. Cover, and refrigerate.

5. Line a shallow serving bowl or high-sided platter with the lettuce leaves. Taste the shrimp mixture for salt, adjust if necessary. Scoop into the prepared bowl and serve, garnished with sprigs of coriander/cilantro or radish roses.

QUESO RELLENO

Stuffed Cheese

Serves 6

1 Edam or Gouda Cheese
(about 2 pounds)
2 pounds ground pork
1 large onion, quartered
2 cloves garlic, peeled
1 teaspoon oregano
1/2 teaspoon salt

Picadillo:
2 onions, minced
2 cloves garlic, mashed
8 large tomatoes, peeled and
chopped
40 golden raisins
40 stuffed green olives,
chopped
2 teaspoons capers
1 cup almonds, blanched and
slivered
1 teaspoon of cinnamon
1 teaspoon allspice
4 hard-cooked eggs, chopped fine
1/2 cup vinegar

Much as I have tried, I cannot find the origin of this dish which is definitely classified as "typically Yucatecan"—obviously, there was a randy, gourmet Hollander somewhere in the ancestral mix!

This either makes a spectacular buffet hors d'oeuvre or a fine entrée when accompanied by hot tortillas to make tacos. Because it's an arduous multistep preparation when done exactly in the Mexican way, I've devised this shorter version—apologies to the many wonderful cooks who have perspired for generations, in the proper confection of the dish.

1. Peel away and discard the red, waxy exterior of the cheese. Cut off in one piece, enough of the top to allow you access. Scoop out all of the cheese, leaving a wall about three-quarter-inch thick. (This is similar to the way you would handle a Halloween Jack-o'-Lantern.)
2. In a large skillet, brown the pork, onion, garlic, oregano, and salt together. Drain away the fat and set the mixture aside.
3. In a large mixing bowl, combine the filling (*picadillo*) ingredients.

4. Divide the filling into 2 parts. Add half to the browned meat mixture and spoon into the hollowed out cheese. Put the cheese "cover" on top and wrap well in cheesecloth. Steam in the top of a double boiler for about 30 minutes.

5. Serve, surrounded with the remaining *Picadillo*, and hot tortillas. Dig in!

Note: Classically, this is also accompanied by kol—*which is a kind of golden gravy made by deglazing the browning skillet with chicken broth and flour, seasoned with saffron for flavor and color. Both sweet and hot chilies can also be added. It's a celebration when someone else is making it, but my way is delicious and less work and cleanup!*

HUEVOS MOTULEÑOS

Eggs, Motul-style

Serves 4

8 corn tortillas
¼ cup vegetable oil
1 large banana, sliced
    diagonally into 8 pieces
1 cup Refried Black Beans
    (substitute canned or see
    recipe, page 28)
¼ cup *Chiltomate* sauce
    (see page 269)
8 eggs, fried in pairs, sunny side up
4 slices of ham, ½-inch thick, cut into 1¼-inch chunks
¾ cup cooked baby peas
¼–½ pound fresh Feta cheese, crumbled

If ever there was a breakfast dish to perk up an indifferent appetite, this exciting way to serve farm-fresh eggs is a treat for the eyes as well as the palate. The brilliant green of the baby peas as they slide around the chunks of red tomato is counterpointed by the snowy cheese and golden fried banana. No festive day is complete in the Yucatán without a heaping order.

1. In a large skillet, fry the tortillas in the hot vegetable oil until just crisp and drain on paper towels. Fry the banana slices in the same oil, drain, and set aside to keep warm.

2. To assemble, spread the refried beans on the tortillas, and top with a pair of fried eggs. Pour the *Chiltomate* sauce over the eggs and surround with the ham, peas, and fried bananas. Garnish with the crumbled cheese and serve at once with additional hot tortillas

PAPADZULES

Yucatecan Egg Tacos

Serves 4

> The cuisine of the Yucatán is other worldly—besides underlining how sophisticated the Mayan civilization was, there is a broad streak of wild nonconformity with other food mores of the Republic. These exquisite tacos are one of the foods I long for when anyone mentions the Yucatán—even the mention of the Mayan word makes me salivate.

3 tablespoons peanut or safflower oil
1 medium-sized onion, chopped
2 cloves garlic, peeled and mashed
1 teaspoon *epazote* leaves (see page 26) or substitute coriander/cilantro
1½ cups raw pumpkin seeds, shelled
2 hot chilies (Habañero, serrano, or Jalapeño) seeded and deveined
2 cups chicken stock
6 hard-cooked eggs, chopped
1 dozen corn tortillas
1 cup **spicy** tomato sauce (purchased hot red sauce)

1. Heat the oil and lightly sauté the onion, garlic, and epazote leaves.
2. Toast the pumpkin seeds in a heavy skillet. (Hold a cover over the pan—the little dickens tend to become ballistic!) In the blender or food processor, quick-grind the toasted seeds, onion, garlic, *epazote*, and chilies, making a sort of paste.
3. In a medium-sized saucepan, add the chicken stock and gradually stir in the pumpkin seed mixture. Allow to simmer until it is a thick, sauce consistency.
4. Fine chop the eggs.
5. Dip each tortilla quickly into the hot oil to soften, then coat on both sides with the pumpkin seed sauce. Place a good dollop of the chopped egg in the center of each and roll, laying each taco seam side down, in an ovenproof casserole.
6. Top with remaining pumpkin seed sauce and pour a stripe of red sauce crosswise over the middle of the tacos.

PAVO PIBIL

Turkey in Annato Sauce

Serves 4

Recado Rojo
(Yield: ¹/₂ cup)
3 tablespoons annato (*achiote*) seeds
1 teaspoon freshly ground black pepper
1 teaspoon salt
1 tablespoon paprika
¹/₂ teaspoon ground cumin
1 teaspoon ground cinnamon
2 tablespoons finely chopped coriander/cilantro and bruised coriander/cilantro
3 cloves garlic, peeled and mashed
juice of 1 orange and 1 lime
1 teaspoon Tabasco, or other hot sauce.
1 tablespoon mild vinegar

The night before:
1. In 1 cup of water, bring the annato seeds to a rolling boil and simmer for 5 minutes. Place in a glass jar with the liquid, cover, and allow to soak overnight.
2. Place annato seeds with their liquid in the blender and blend to a smooth paste. Add the 5 dry spices, the coriander/cilantro, garlic, orange and lime juice, and Tabasco. Blend well. Remove from blender jar,[1] scrape into a glass bowl or jar, and if it is too thick to spread (it should be peanut-butter consistency), add up to 1 tablespoon of vinegar.

Pibil *derives from the Mayan word for roasting pits. The flavor of the spicy red sauce,* Recado Rojo, *lends particular culinary subtlety to fowl and pork. Try to prepare this in double batches and allow it to season for several days in a glass jar in the refrigerator. It will last indefinitely in the freezer.*

Turkey is enjoyed everywhere in the Southeast and here you find it Pibil-style. Instead of the Mexican "papillote"— (steamed in banana leaves), I Americanize the preparation and steam-bake it in aluminum foil—easy and no pots to wash!

Note: *In Los Almendros restaurant in Ticúl it will be served with the local beverage specialty* Xtabentum *(pronounced: shtah-bent-oom). The masterful melding of honey, anise, and Xtabentum flowers is delicious!*

---

[1] If your blender has a plastic jar, it will be a lovely shade of orange. Annato is a common vegetable dye used in the U.S. to color cheese. Don't despair, this fades after several turns in the dishwasher.

To assemble:
3–4 pound turkey breast
3 tablespoons vegetable oil
3 large red onions, thinly sliced
2 large cloves garlic, minced
1 tablespoon oregano
juice of 6 limes
zest of 2 oranges
2 slices bacon, cut in half

1. On both sides of the turkey breast bone, cut the meat away in a solid chunk. Divide each chunk in half lengthwise again. Rub and coat each of the 4 pieces well with the annato paste (*recado*). Wrap in foil and allow to marinate in the refrigerator for several hours or overnight.
2. Heat the oil and sauté the onions and garlic until limp. Set aside.
3. Cut 4 large (12 x 12-inch) pieces of aluminum foil. Place one marinated turkey breast in the middle of each piece of foil. Sprinkle with oregano. Top with the onion, garlic mixture, lime juice, and orange zest, with a half slice of bacon on top. Wrap the foil tightly so that the cooking steam will not escape.
4. In 325°F oven, bake for 2–2½ hours.
5. Serve in the just-opened foil, garnished with citrus slices, and accompanied by pickled onions.

PATO SILVESTRE "PUUC"

Wild Duck, Yucatecan-style

Serves 6

6 small wild ducks (6 Cornish
    hens, may be substituted)
2 onions, peeled and cut into
    1/2-inch chunks
4 carrots, unpeeled and cut
    into 1/2-inch chunks
1/2 cup chopped celery leaves
    and stems
handful of parsley leaves
1 clove garlic

Sauce:
1 cup almonds, blanched and
    ground
2 cloves garlic, peeled
1/2 teaspoon cumin
1 egg yolk, well beaten
1–2 tablespoons vegetable oil
sprigs of fresh mint

The hills of Puuc are a rolling relief to the otherwise flat Yucatecan peninsula. The site of the spectacular Uxmal ruins and other smaller archeologic sites, the jungle scrub offers haven and sustenance for flocks of wild ducks.

This recipe reflects the culinary influences of the Middle Eastern immigrants (Arabic and Lebanese) who settled in Mérida; descendants of the adventurers and seekers of fortune who sailed to the New World on Spanish ships in continuation of Islam's conquest of Western Europe.

1. Clean the fowl well, inside and out, singe, and truss. Place in a large pot or Dutch oven, cover with boiling water, and cook for 10 minutes. (This is not necessary with Cornish hens.) Drain, discarding liquid.
2. Cover with fresh boiling water and add the onions, carrots, celery leaves, parsley, and whole garlic clove. Cook until the fowl is tender,[1] 10–15 minutes. Cool in the stock and let stand overnight.
3. Remove the fowl from the liquid, reserving the stock. Fifteen minutes before serving, drain and dry. Preheat the oven to 450°F.

---

[1] Cooking time varies according to what kind of fowl you are using.

4. Place the ducks on a rack in a broiling pan, brush with vegetable oil, and roast for 10–15 minutes, turning until brown and "crackly-skinned" on all sides.

5. To prepare the almond sauce, mix the almonds, minced garlic, and cumin in a blender, grinder, or minichopper. Blend in the egg yolks. In medium-sized saucepan, sauté the mixture for 3 minutes. Add 1½ cups of duck stock, stirring well to incorporate the flavors. Cover and keep on a very low flame. Place the fowl on heated plates (serve whole if you are using the small, wild variety, or carve into appropriate serving pieces), with hot almond sauce. Garnish with sprigs of fresh mint.

RECADO DE CHILMOLE
(RELLENO NEGRO)

. . . .

Yucatecan Black Sauce

Yields: 1–1½ cups

1 tablespoon annato seeds
1 tablespoon each, lemon and
   orange juice
½ cup tequila (vodka may be
   substituted)
1 pound of dried ancho chile
4 whole allspice
2 whole cloves
¼ teaspoon cumin
1 tablespoon of black pepper
8 good-sized garlic cloves,
   peeled
1 teaspoon dried oregano
1 teaspoon salt
lemon or grapefruit juice

1. In a small bowl, soak the annato seeds in the citrus juices, covered, overnight.
2. Follow the general instruction for preparing dried chilies (see pages 174–175). Move away from the stove (tequila is ignitable) and sprinkle tequila over the rinsed, seeded, and deveined, dried chilies.

Recado, is a funny word—it translates literally as "message," and savoring this black velvety sauce perhaps does indeed send the message to the brain, that says, "get ready tongue and taste buds, here comes something wonderful."

The Yucatán makes several recados. The common red variety (recipe page 264), a simple, dusty-chartreuse-colored recado (Recado Para Bistec) which is used for seasoning soups, seafood, and strangely enough, beef, and then this exotic favorite of mine and several others, unique to each cook's repertoire.

This recipe is an adaptation from the Comida Yucateca issue of the splendid magazine, Mexico Desconocido. First, visit a Latin American or Caribbean ethnic food store to secure the ancho chilies.

Continued

3. Allow the chilies to sit for enough time to allow the liquor to be absorbed. Toast the chilies on a griddle, or in a large, nonstick frypan turning frequently, until they are very black. Remove from the griddle or pan, place them in a sieve, and rinse them in hot water. Drain.

4. In a food processor, grind the annato seeds. (They are very hard, so "pulse" them to keep your grinder or blender from burning out). Blend with the rest of the ingredients. Add lemon or orange juice if necessary to get a putty like consistency. Put the recado in a glass jar and allow to season for several days in the refrigerator. It will keep indefinitely.

Now, I want to warn you that this is a rainy day recipe that requires about an hour and a half prep time, staying with the ingredients throughout the various stages. The other side of the coin, is that this flavoring paste is not available commercially here, therefore, I always double the recipe—it keeps for ages.

If actually working with the ingredients is not your thing, at least you'll be able to order from a menu intelligently on your next trip to Mexico.

Note: The uses of the recados are endless, and you can't make any mistakes. Whatever tastes good to you is acceptable. I like poached chicken breasts with this one, served with plain white rice and garnished with the traditional slices of hard-cooked eggs and a few crunchy radishes.

Another savory way to enjoy this zesty recado is to toss it with lean ground pork and a cup of bread cubes and use it as a stuffing for a roasting fowl.

OF
TOMATOES,
RED AND GREEN

Did you know that the tomato (g. lycopersicon) is a member of the nightshade family; was discovered to be edible in Mexico, and is the most utilized fruit/vegetable (take your pick) in the world? That's hardly classifiable as trivia when it forms such an integral part of international cuisine!

Mexico's pre-Columbian inhabitants were responsible for the cultivation and eventual dissemination (through the clergy and the conquistadores) of several dozen, until then unknown, food products.

Documented are the avocado, sesame seeds, peanuts, cocoa, sweet potatoes, chili peppers, corn, beans, potatoes, and tomatoes.

Tomatoes in Mexico are of three basic varieties; the true round, red, juicy beauty so well known to all of us *(jitomate bola)*, the Italian plum-type *(tomate guajillo)*, and the no-relation, little green tomatillo *(tomate verde)*.

Because we are so familiar with both red varieties, let's pause to make friends with the adopted cousin in the family. Variously called in English: "tomatillo," "husk tomato," "cape gooseberry," and by our own American Indian names of "ground cherry" and "strawberry tomato." The sub species name, for those of you who keep track of obscure facts, is g. *physalis pubescens*.

There is no Mexican cuisine without the small, green vegetable which wears a parchment-like overcoat. Never eaten raw (bite into one and you'll discover why!), they are most often stewed or prefried for sauces. In long-cooking *moles*, they are first sautéed to release the flavor and then set to stew to meld the flavors, for several hours or days. As with most growing things, they also have wide medicinal use. This is an anecdote about my first introduction to the omnipresence of the *tomate verde* in the Mexican household.

Recently arrived in Mexico City, my greatest desire was to be "accepted" by my Mexican friends. One of the strange and exotic things I noticed was that every Latin female had her ears pierced. Remember that this was the early 1950's, and our own youngsters were not puncturing their audio-protective cartilage in numerous places with the abandon of today. (I was later enthusiastically, to have my little Mexican-born, daughter's ears perforated in the hospital right after delivery, as was the custom.)

Here I was, a married lady and a mother, and I still had "virgin" ears. A friendly neighbor suggested she pierce them for me, and always the adventurer, I agreed. "No duele nada!" ("It doesn't hurt at all!"), she assured, and it didn't. But several days after she had sterilized my darning needle and drawn the dental floss through my lobes, both ears looked like inverted giant lollipops— and how they throbbed!

After a dozen trips to charming Dr. Reyes, and the *farmacia* for potions and lotions and creams and elixirs, all to no avail, my Indian cook cocked her head at me and said: "Las puedo curar, se me permite?" (I can fix them—if you let me.)

She marched me into the kitchen and husked and cut in half a fat, little tomatillo, dropped the cut sides down on the hot comal (a small, galvanized griddle "de rigueur" in Mexican kitchens— used mostly to heat tortillas), and let them sizzle. She then placed one-half on each ear lobe and told me to lie down holding on to my vegetable earmuffs. Pressing the warm pulp against the wounds, I fell asleep.

Waking an hour later—the throbbing had stopped, the swelling had diminished by half, and after several repetitions of the homeopathic remedy, I replaced the stained floss with tiny, jewel studs.

In later years, I used the warmed juice of the *tomates* as an acne palliative for my teenagers and it worked equally well. Witchcraft, folk medicine, or faith—I reasoned, if we can eat them, they certainly can't do any external harm, and like chicken soup "it can't hurt!"

ESCABECHE CAMPECHANO

Pickled Fish, Campeche-style

Serves 6

The Miramar restaurant in Campeche City is not elegant, but the chilled pickled fish served with small, hot, boiled potatoes, is—enjoy your dinner and then take a walk around the old sea walls (Baluartes) and dream of the colonial elegance that once marked this now slowly deteriorating seaport.

2 pounds firm white fish, thickly sliced
juice of 1 lime
2 tablespoons salt
1 tablespoon Tabasco sauce
$\frac{1}{2}$ cup wine vinegar
3 large red onions, thickly sliced
1 cup olive oil
5 cloves garlic
10 black peppercorns
$\frac{1}{2}$ teaspoon oregano
2 bay leaves
1 teaspoon allspice

1. Wash the fish slices and soak for 10 minutes in enough water to cover mixed with the lime juice and 1 tablespoon of salt.

2. Dissolve the Tabasco and 1 teaspoon of salt in the vinegar. Soak the onions in boiling water to which 1 teaspoon of salt has been added, drain, and soak in the Tabasco mixture for 15 minutes. Remove, reserving the onions and vinegar.

3. In a large, heavy skillet, heat the olive oil and fry 2 whole cloves of garlic until they are browned. Discard the garlic. Add the fish, peppercorns, oregano, bay leaves, allspice, the rest of the garlic, chopped, and the reserved vinegar. **Do not** add water. Simmer over low heat for 15 minutes. Place in the refrigerator in a glass container and chill. Before serving remove the bay leaves.

4. Serve cold, garnished with onion and lime slices.

Sauce is at the base of every wonderful Yucatecan dish. Elsewhere on these pages you will find several regional sauces accompanying recipes. The Chiltomate *and* Xni Pec *(isn't that a lovely Mayan word?) sit colorfully side by side on tables all over the peninsula.*

SALSA DE CHILTOMATE

. . . .

Yucatecan Tomato Sauce

Yield: 1–1$^1/_2$ cups

4 large, ripe tomatoes, peeled and blanched
4–5 Habañero chiles, seared, with seeds and veins
    removed
1 large, sweet onion, grated
1 large bunch cilantro, minced
salt, to taste

Grind or mash all of the ingredients together, taking great care with the Habañero chilies, they are devils! You can substitute Serranos or Jalapeños with good results. Place in a glass dish. Refrigerate until meal time or this will ferment.

XNI PEC
(SHNEE-PECK)

. . . .

Use the above ingredients, substituting raw plum tomatoes, and coarse chop rather than grind. Add one-half cup of vinegar or lemon juice.

LOMITOS DE CERDO VALLADOLID

Very Spicy Pork with Beans

Serves 6

2 cups dried black beans, sorted
  and rinsed
2 quarts water
1 teaspoon vegetable oil
½ onion
4 tablespoons vegetable oil
2 pounds boneless pork, cut
  into 1-inch chunks
4 cups chicken broth
4 large tomatoes, skinned and
  chopped
2 sprigs *epazote* (see page 26)
  or
  1 teaspoon dried
6–8 dried serrano chilies or 1 tablespoon of chili powder
1 tablespoon salt
8 radishes, finely chopped (optional)
2 hard-cooked eggs, quartered

1. Place the beans in a large pot, add the water, 1 teaspoon of vegetable oil, and the onion, and bring to a rolling boil for 10 minutes. Lower the heat to medium, and continue cooking, covered, for 1 hour. Drain the beans, reserving the liquid.

2. Heat 4 tablespoons of vegetable oil in a heavy skillet with a cover. Add the beans, pork, chicken broth, tomatoes, *epazote*, and chilies. Cook, covered, over medium heat, for another hour. If too much liquid cooks off, add up to 2 cups more broth. Add the salt and cook for 30 minutes. Adjust the seasonings.

3. Serve in a large, preheated tureen or casserole dish, garnished with the finely chopped radishes, and the hard-cooked egg quarters.

Don't miss a magical swim in the subterranean wonderland that is the sacred Cenote Dzitnup. *It is said that there are small, blind fish here who were the guides to the Mayan netherworld—unfortunately I've never met anyone who's seen the perhaps-mythical swimmers.*

This dish, served with steamy tortillas, makes a great lunch after your early morning adventure. It is particularly savory served in the flowered patio and quiet of the Mesón del Marqués.

TORTA DEL CIELO

Heavenly Almond Cake

Serves 8–10

1 pound of almonds, peeled
   and chopped fine
1 tablespoon flour
½ teaspoon baking powder
10 eggs, separated
½ teaspoon cream of tartar
1 pound sugar
1 teaspoon vanilla
1 teaspoon cognac
confectioners' sugar, for garnish

Yucatán is almond country. The umbrella-like shape of the almond trees affording welcome shade in this tropical clime. This simple-to-make, but rich dessert is a favorite at all "Fiestas Yucatecas." The recipe is translated from Comida Yucateca, Guía Gastronómica-México Desconocido.

1. Spray a round, 12-inch cake pan with liquid shortening. Cut a circle of waxed paper the same size, lay it in the bottom of the pan, and spray it also.
2. Blend the almonds with the flour and baking powder, and set aside. Heat the oven to 375°F.
3. In a large bowl, beat the egg whites with the cream of tartar until they form soft peaks . . . continue beating, incorporating the sugar a little at a time, until hard, glossy peaks are formed.
4. Add the yolks one by one, continuing to beat gently. Add the vanilla and cognac. Empty into the cake pan and bake for 40–45 minutes or until the top is nicely browned.
5. Remove from the oven to a cooling rack and allow to cool for 5 minutes. Unmold to a serving platter and allow to cool completely. Dust with powdered sugar before presenting.

PONCHE DELICIOSO YUCATECO

Yucatecan Fruit Punch

Serves 6

3 cups milk
3 eggs
4 tablespoons of corn syrup
3 tablespoons brown sugar
4 bananas
1 cup rum
1/8 teaspoon ground nutmeg
1 cup shaved ice
6 strawberries for garnish

1. Put the whole shebang in a blender and let 'er rip! Serve in tall glasses with a strawberry on top.

There are no more spectacular sunsets than those of the Sureste. Sprawled in a double hammock swaying under a palapa (palm frond roof), snap your fingers and perhaps an attentive Mayan genie will pop out of a bottle and bring you one of these frothy coolers. They masquerade under many names, so simply ask for the daily Ponche de frutas.

BIBLIOGRAPHY

Artes de Mexico, issues #'s 107, 108. Compiled by Jaime Saldívar. *La Cocina Méxicana II*, Mexico City. 1968.

_____, #121. *El Dulce en México*, Mexico City 1969.

Bayless, Rick, with Deann Groen Bayless. *Authentic Mexican: Regional Cooking from the Heart of Mexico*. New York, William Morrow and Company, Inc.

Benítez, Ana M. *Pre-Hispanic Cooking/Cocina Prehispánica*. Mexico City: Ediciones Euroamericanas Klaus Thiele, 1974.

Bruns, Rebecca. *Hidden Mexico*, Berkeley, California, Ulysses Press 1987.

Carbia, Maria A. de. *Mexico Through My Kitchen Window*, Houghton Mifflin Co. Boston 1961.

_____ *México en la Cocina de Marichú*, Mexico City: Editorial Epoca, 1944.

Condon, Richard/Bennett, Wendy. *The Mexican Stove—What to Put On It and In It*, Doubleday & Co. Garden City, NY. 1973.

Díaz del Castillo, Bernal, *The Conquest of New Spain*, translated and edited by J. M. Cohen. Baltimore: Penguin Books, 1963.

Embassy Women's Group of the Embassy of the United States of America. *El Cookbook*, Mexico City, 1977.

Farga, Amando. *Eating in Mexico*, Mexican Restaurant Association, Mexico City, 1963.

Farga Font, José. *Cocina Veracruzana y de Tabasco, Campeche y Yucatán*, Editores Méxicanos Unidos, México D.F. 1974.

_____ *Historia de la Comida en México*, José Inés Loredo y José Luis Loredo. Mexico City 1968.

Gabilondo, Aída. *Mexican Family Cooking*. New York: Fawcett Columbine, 1986.

Iturriaga de la Fuente. José N. *De Tacos, Tamales y Tortas*. Mexico City: Editorial Diana, 1987.

Junior League of Mexico, Buén Provecho, Mexico City, 1981.

Kennedy, Diana. *The Cuisines of Mexico*. New York: Harper & Row, 1972.

Recipes from the Regional Cooks of Mexico. New York: Harper & Row, 1978.

Lomelí, Arturo. *El Chili y Otros Picantes*, Mexico City, Editorial Prometeo Libre, 1986.

MacMiadhachain, Anna and Aaron, Jan. *Spanish & Mexican Cooking*, Octopus Books Ltd. London, 1979.

México Desconocido, *Comida Yucateca*, Editorial Jilguero, SA de CV, Mexico, D.F.

El Maíz, *Fundamento de la Cultura Popular Mexicana*. Mexico City, Museo de Culturas Populares, 1987.

Martínez, Zarela. *Food From My Heart*, Macmillan Publishing, New York 1992.

Molinar, Rita. *Dulces Mexicanos*, Mexico City, Editorial Pax-Mexicano, 1981.

Mulvey, Ruth Watt & Alvarez, Luisa María. *Good Food from Mexico*, New York, M. Barrows and Co. 1958.

Novo, Salvador. *Historia Gastronómica de la Ciudad de México*, Editorial Porrua, S.A., Mexico City 1979.

Quintana, Patricia. Chapter Introductions: William A. Orme Jr., *The Taste of Mexico*, Stewart, Tabori & Chang, New York 1986.

Rivera, Virginia Rodríguez. *La Comida en el México Antiquo y Moderno*, Mexico City, Editorial Pormaca, 1965.

Soustelle, Jacques. *México, Tierra India*, Mexico City, Secretaría de Educación Pública, primera edición en español 1971.

Spieler, Marlena. *Flavors of Mexico*, Los Angeles, California, Lowell House, 1991.

Thompson, Katherine & Charlotte. *Cadogan Guides—Mexico*, Cadogan Books London, Globe Pequot Press, Chester Conn. 1991.

Toor, Frances. *A Treasury of Mexican Folkways*. New York: Bonanza Books.

Unknown. Libro de Cosina en Que Se Da La Razón de los Beneficios de Cada Cosa, y Sus Compuestos, Productos Metálicos Standard, SA Mexico 1987.

Velasquez de León, Josefine. *Cocina Veracruzana*, Mexico City, Editorial Universo Mexico, 1988.

___ , La Cocina Española en México, Editorial Universo, Mexico. 1990.

Women's Association of Union Church, Mexico City. *American Design for Cooking in Mexico*, Mexico City, 1951.

INDEX

HEALTHY MEXICAN REGIONAL COOKERY

HEALTHY MEXICAN REGIONAL COOKERY